Gifts

Finding the Spiritual Gifts that God Has Placed In You

by
Susan J. Rogers

Tulsa, OK

19 18 17 16 15   10 9 8 7 6 5 4 3 2 1

Gifts
Finding the Spiritual Gifts that God Has Placed In You
ISBN: 978-168031-015-3
Copyright © 2015 by Susan J. Rogers

Published by:
Harrison House Publishers
Tulsa, OK 74145
www.harrisonhouse.com

TABLE OF CONTENTS

ACKNOWLEDGMENTS

This book is dedicated to the Holy Spirit who has anointed my tongue the pen of a ready writer.

To Thornwell, my husband, whose love and support brought God's dream for my life into reality.

A special thanks to my beautiful children Clint and Tiffany, who sacrificed our time together to allow me to fulfill another one of God's dreams for my life.

I want to express my sincere and loving appreciation to Dr. Leanna Hall and Thornwell for their time, effort and expertise in editing, and to Carol McGinnis for typing this manuscript.

Foreword

With great pleasure, today I write this foreword for Susan Rogers' book, *Gifts*. I have known this book for many years and have always felt it was well written and backed up with superb explanations of the Greek. One thing that often bothers me is when people use the Greek, but do so with great misinterpretation. In *Gifts*, Susan has backed up what she teaches based on the New Testament Greek language in a very professional manner. Not only do I recommend this book, but I have used this book as I have taught my own congregation about the gifts of the Spirit and the various enabling graces of God for the Church.

I pray this book is a blessing to you as it has been to me.

Rick Renner
Rick Renner Ministries

INTRODUCTION

Have these questions ever crossed your mind: Was I created for a purpose? Can I do something for the Lord? Am I special to God? If these questions or others like them have ever crossed your mind, then this book was written for you.

Yes! You were created for a purpose, and that purpose was for the Father God's pleasure (Revelation 4:11). The Father God created you for a special plan that was generated by the Godhead. God the Father has designed a plan for your life that no one else can execute but you. He had you in mind before the foundations of the earth.

For we are his workmanship, created in Christ Jesus unto good works, which God hath before ordained that we should walk in them.

Ephesians 2:10

God has endowed you with gifts, talents, and abilities enabling you to accomplish His will on earth for your life. So many believers stop here and say they can't do anything for God. "I'm not creative, I can't sing; or I'm not a teacher or pastor." I have great news for you. God is not looking at your natural ability. He created you and gave you supernatural ability. He's looking for believers who realize that the greater One (Jesus Christ) lives within them and through Jesus Christ, they are willing to yield and respond to His ability in them to accomplish God's will on earth.

This book covers what you need to know on how to make God's gifts, talents, and abilities operable in your life.

Time is a valuable entity. We can use it wisely for God's glory or we can misuse it and lose it for eternity. When you work for the King of kings, He will redeem your time (Colossians 4:5). This book is designed to help believers find their place in the body of Christ so their time can be used wisely.

Did you know God gave you part of His personality in a gift that will motivate you toward your office (ministry) in the body of Christ? Let's get started so you can find out who you are in Christ and what God's purpose is for your life.

The time has now come for the body of Christ to take responsibility for its' life, realizing that individually we will stand before our Lord and Savior Jesus Christ and answer for what we have done in our lifetime (2 Corinthians 5:10).

1

CREATED FOR A PURPOSE

Contrary to most humans' belief that man was created for his own pleasure, Revelation 4:11 reveals to us that God created mankind for His pleasure.

> **Thou art worthy, O Lord, to receive glory and honour and power: for thou hast created all things, and FOR THY PLEASURE THEY ARE AND WERE CREATED (emphasis mine).**

God created mankind to serve Him (Ephesians 2:10). Jesus Christ, our example said: "...but whosoever will be great among you, let him be your minister; And whosoever will be chief among you, let him be your servant: Even as the Son of man came not to be ministered unto, but to minister, and to give his life a ransom for many" (Matthew 20:26-28). Jesus gave His life as a servant.

Upon salvation, the believer receives a *gift of grace* (Romans 12:6-8). Included in this gift is a part of God's personality. This gift of grace motivates believers toward their ministry office(s)(1 Corinthians 12:28) in the body of Christ. Let's see how the gifts of grace motivated believers in the New Testament toward their ministry gifts.

John the Baptist had the gift of grace of prophecy, which motivated him toward his ministry offices of prophet, teacher, and evangelist (1 Corinthians 12:28 and Ephesians 4: 11). A prophet is a God-inspired speaker proclaiming a divine message regarding the mind and counsel of God.

The person with the gift of grace of prophecy is direct, frank, abhors evil, and cannot tolerate people continuing in sin. John the Baptist had God's viewpoint on sin and a part of God's personality in his gift of grace of prophecy. This does not mean everyone with the gift of grace of prophecy will be a prophet. Absolutely NOT! This is an example of how the gift of grace of prophecy worked in John the Baptist, producing unique effects that accomplished God's will for his life. God called John the Baptist as a prophet to proclaim His truth on the area of sin.

Another example would be Paul, who had also received the gift of grace of prophecy (Romans 12:6) which motivated him toward his ministry offices of apostle, prophet, evangelist, pastor and teacher in the body of Christ. Paul also received a part of God's personality in his gift of grace of prophecy. Paul's offices were fulfilled by his yielding and submitting to the greater one within him. Over the years, I have heard Paul used as an example of an exhorter and teacher when the gifts of grace have been taught. Paul was a great exhorter and teacher, but the gift of grace that motivated him was prophecy. His ability to correct and instruct the body of Christ (directed by the Holy Spirit) came from his gift of grace of prophecy. He had God's viewpoint on sin. In order for you to get a clear picture of Paul's gift of grace, let's look at a particular example that clarifies prophecy as his motivation. In 1 Corinthians chapter 5, Paul instructs the church of Corinth on how to deal with a particular fornicator in their church. He instructs them in verse 9 not only to disassociate with the believer who is the fornicator at this time but also to get him out of their church (verse 13).

Like we previously stated, prophecy is direct, frank, and abhors evil. Paul hated sin because of his gift of grace of prophecy. If Paul had the gift of grace of exhortation, he would have exhorted them to encourage this particular believer to repent. An exhorter would have never ordered a believer to be exiled. If Paul had the gift of grace of teaching, he would have explained biblically the scriptural procedure on how to deal with fornication. But Paul had the gift of grace of prophecy as we can see by his demanding a quick removal of the believer, regardless of his actions or feelings. It was not until he had time to consider this problem before God that he changed his mind. In 2 Corinthians, chapter 2, we see that Paul realized that he had been too tough on the fornicator and that God's mercy endures forever. If that man truly repented, then it would have been unfair not to forgive him and reinstate him in their church.

Paul instructs the church of Corinth to reinstate this man and forgive him of his sin. In verse 7, Paul says to comfort him so he won't give up in his discouragement. Paul came from God's judgmental side (prophecy) and had not been fair with this particular believer who had repented from his sin of fornication. Paul says he forgave in the Person of Christ by yielding to the greater one (Jesus Christ) in him.

Peter is an excellent example of a person motivated by the gift of grace of exhortation. The gift of grace of exhortation motivated Peter toward his ministry offices of apostle, evangelist, pastor and teacher.

And with MANY OTHER WORDS did he testify and exhort, saying, Save yourselves from this untoward generation.

Acts 2:40

The gift of grace of exhortation is given by God to stimulate faith. On the day of Pentecost, Peter stimulated faith and 3,000 souls were added to the Kingdom. They were not only saved but also baptized and verse 42 of Acts chapter 2 says they continued with the apostles' doctrine. Exhorters stimulate faith and encourage believers to live a life pleasing to God.

Exhorters also have a great love and faith in the Lord Jesus Christ (Philemon 5). Peter's example of his love towards Jesus is found in John 21:15-17. Peter was grieved because the Lord had asked him three times if he loved Him. His comment, "...Lord you know all things..." reveals his defense. An example of Peter's faith in Jesus is found in Matthew chapter 14. Peter was the only disciple who exercised faith in the Lord Jesus Christ when he stepped out of the boat onto the water.

Peter's comments in his second letter let us know he exhorted and stimulated faith in believers until his death.

> **Wherefore I will not be negligent to put you ALWAYS IN REMEMBRANCE of these things, though ye know them, and be ESTABLISHED in the PRESENT TRUTH.** Yea, I think it meet, **as long as I am in this tabernacle, TO STIR YOU UP by putting you in remembrance; knowing that shortly I must put off this my tabernacle, even as our Lord Jesus Christ hath showed me.**
>
> **2 Peter 1:12-14, (emphasis mine)**

Notice in verse 12 that Peter says he would not be negligent to put believers in remembrance of God's Word. The reason for that was his desire to see believers become established in God's truths. He did not want believers to become deceived by being hearers only (James 1:22).

These and additional examples on the relationships of spiritual gifts will be given in chapter 3. The gifts of grace found in Romans 12:6-8 motivate believers toward their ministry office(s) found in 1 Corinthians 12:28 and/or Ephesians 4:11. This book was not only written to show believers their importance but also their potential in God. The following chapters define every spiritual gift listed in the Bible and will stimulate believers to use them.

DON'T SETTLE FOR LESS THAN
GOD'S BEST FOR YOUR LIFE!

REMEMBER: YOU HAVE BEEN CREATED
FOR THE FATHER'S PLEASURE.

2

WHAT DOES A SPIRITUAL GIFT ENCOMPASS?

This book covers each spiritual gift found in the New Testament and shows how God intended for them to work together.

THE DEFINITION OF A SPIRITUAL GIFT IS:

GOD-GIVEN ABILITY to function effectively IN A PARTICULAR SERVICE to BENEFIT A MEMBER(S) of the body of Christ.

The three main parts to a spiritual gift are:

1. A God-given ability

2. Service

3. Recipient

The intrinsic characteristics of a spiritual gift are God's ability, strength and power.

Not that we are sufficient of ourselves to think any-thing as of ourselves; but our sufficiency is of God.

2 Corinthians 3:5

This scripture is indispensable to the believer. "Sufficient" used here in the Greek means to arrive whereas "sufficiency" means ability. Let's take a closer look at this scripture and see what Paul is telling us.

Not that we have arrived in ourselves to think anything of ourselves; but our ability is of God (my paraphrase).

A GOD-GIVEN ABILITY

When you receive a spiritual gift, God equips you with every-thing you will need to operate in it. Instantaneously you inherit God's ability, strength and power. In the Greek, God's ability, strength and power are collectively interwoven. To further explain this, let's look at the story of Samson found in Judges chapters 13 through 16. This story will help you understand how God's ability is tied to His strength and displayed through His power. Without God's ability and strength, Samson was powerless, as was the case when Delilah cut his hair. He lost his strength, leaving him powerless until God renewed it one last time. This renewal resulted in a display of God's power that destroyed the Philistine's palace along with thousands of men and women. This shows how God's ability and strength are displayed through His power. Let's look at another scripture that makes this clearer.

**For it is God which worketh in you both to will and
to do of his good pleasure.**

Philippians 2:13

When you receive a spiritual gift, then God's ability, strength
and power immediately start to work in you to accomplish God's
will. "Worketh" here in the Greek is defined as God's energizing,
active and operative power. Our English word "energy" is derived
from this word. God's energizing power is what activates and operates His spiritual gifts working through the believer.

FUNCTIONING IN YOUR GIFT

The second part of a spiritual gift is functioning in your particular service. Service is an activity on behalf of a person or group. The
four lists of spiritual gift (Romans 12:6-8; Ephesians 4:11; 1 Corinthians 12:7-9, 28) that will be studied in this book detail giftsgiven
by God to serve the body of Christ. There are varied reasons for the
different spiritual gifts as will be discussed in the following chapters.

I want you to notice that these gifts are given to serve the body
of Christ. This is God's way of meeting the spiritual and practical
needs of His children.

**And he gave some, apostles; and some, prophets;
and some, evangelists; and some, pastors and teachers; for the perfecting of the saints, for the edifying
of the body of Christ.**

Ephesians 4: 11, 12

This list of spiritual gifts found in Ephesians 4:11,12 details
gifts given for the perfecting of the saints. "Perfecting" is *katartismos*

in the Greek meaning completely furnish and/or to prepare. This list is commonly known as the five-fold ministry offices. However, it is noteworthy that this is a partial list of ministry offices that correlates with a list found in 1 Corinthians 12:28. The reason for the separation of these two lists is their difference in purpose. The five-fold ministry offices are given to the body of Christ for the perfecting (maturing) of the body of Christ whereas the list found in 1 Corinthians 12:28 details gifts given for the aid and support of the church. Let's see how these ministry offices meet the spiritual needs of believers and serve the body of Christ.

Paul tells us these spiritual gifts are given by Jesus Christ for the perfecting of the saints. The second part of Ephesians 4:12 says they are for the work of the ministry. "Work" here in the Greek is defined as to toil as an effort or occupation. Notice in the definition of work it says "occupation" and the reason being are that these gifts are full time positions. The manifestations of the Holy Spirit (1 Corinthians 12:7-11) are for a brief period of time, whereas the gifts of grace motivate believers toward their office(s). But the five ministry offices in Ephesians 4:11 are a way of life.

The last part of Ephesians 4:12 tells us these gifts are for the edifying of the body of Christ. The Body of Christ refers to all Christians collectively. "Edifying" in the Greek means architecture or structure. Edifying is therefore an act of promoting spiritual growth by building upon the believer's foundation, which is Jesus Christ. Paul is telling us these spiritual gifts listed in Ephesians 4:11 are to equip the body of Christ by fully preparing them for their work in God's Kingdom. Once you receive Jesus Christ as your personal Lord and Savior, you no longer live for yourself.

I am crucified with Christ: nevertheless I live; yet not I, but Christ liveth in me: and the life which I now live in the flesh I live by the faith of the Son of God, who loved me, and gave himself for me.

Galatians 2:20

The responsibility of individuals having one or more of the five-fold ministry offices in Ephesians 4: 11 is to fully prepare believers for their calling (ministry office) found in 1 Corinthians 12:28.

Every believer has at least one of the ministry offices (gifts) found in Corinthians 12:28 as will be discussed in chapter 3. However, the five-fold ministry offices found in Ephesians 4:11 are limited, which will also be discussed in chapter 3. We all have different life callings from God. Some are called as pastors, evangelists, and prophets while others are called as choir members, Sunday school teachers, nursery workers, church janitors, etc. Whatever ministry God calls you to serve in, you are required to do it as unto the Lord (Colossians 3:23, 24).

Even so ye, forasmuch as ye are zealous of spiritual gifts, seek that ye may excel to the edifying of the church.

1 Corinthians 14: 12

Edifying used in this scripture is the same word as found in Ephesians 4:12. God's desire is to see His Church grow spiritually. Edifying, as we saw earlier, is the act of promoting spiritual growth by building upon the believer's foundation (salvation). This only comes from stepping out and using the spiritual gifts that have been entrusted to you. Paul says, "Ye are zealous of spiritual gifts, seek that ye may excel to the edifying of the church. "Zealous" in the Greek means covet earnestly and/or intense or eager interest. He's telling us that being interested in spiritual gifts is important but we should seek to excel in edifying the Church. Promoting spiritual growth in other believers comes from stepping out and doing your work in the ministry.

> **From whom the whole body fitly joined together and compacted by that which every joint supplieth, according to the effectual working in the measure of every part, maketh increase of the body unto the edifying of itself in love.**
>
> **Ephesians 4:16**

God expects every believer to commit to a church and get involved. "Every joint supplieth" makes it clear that every believer has a responsibility to get involved in serving the Lord. Ministry offices (1 Corinthians 12:28 and Ephesians 4:11) are found in the church, as will be discussed in chapter 14. Spiritual gifts are given by God to serve the body of Christ as a whole. They are not for the personal use of the individual who receives them. We can see in the scripture above that each believer stepping up to take responsibility for his part or work in God's plan will result in the growth and maturity of the body as it is built up in love.

In review, it is the responsibility of the ministry offices (Ephesians 4:11) to fully prepare the saints for their work in the ministry.

Then it becomes the believer's responsibility to supply their "joint" by stepping out and accepting their God-given office (ministry), resulting in the spiritual growth of the body of Christ (Ephesians 4:16).

RECIPIENT

The last part of a spiritual gift is the recipient who benefits from others' operation of the gift. God's spiritual gifts are given to the body of Christ to benefit others. Believers who have received spiritual gifts are also beneficiaries of God's blessings. However, the purpose of spiritual gifts is to benefit others, as confirmed in Paul's statement in 1 Corinthians 12:7:

But the manifestation of the Spirit is given to every man to <u>PROFIT WITHAL</u> (emphasis mine).

The manifestations of the Holy Spirit, commonly known as the "charismatic gifts," are *phanerosis* in the Greek. This scripture reveals the purpose of the manifestations are to profit withal meaning that these spiritual gifts are given to benefit others in the body of Christ.

We previously studied Ephesians 4:11, 12 which further substantiated that these spiritual gifts are to benefit others in the body of Christ. The five-fold ministry gifts prepare believers for their work in the ministry, resulting in the entire body of Christ being blessed by spiritual growth.

As every man hath received the gift, even so minister the same one to another, as good stewards of the manifold grace of God.

1 Peter 4: 10

The "gift" that is mentioned here is defined in the Greek as a spiritual endowment. This verse is not referring specifically to any of the mentioned in the four lists of spiritual gifts but rather in generality to any spiritual gift (talent or ability). Peter tells us as you have received a spiritual endowment from God, even so, minister one to another. "Minister" in the Greek means to serve others as an attendant and/or waiter. This verse further confirms that the purpose of a spiritual gift is to benefit others.

BENEFITS TO THE BELIEVER:

Responsibility is a major part of our stewardship. It is obvious that when we receive a spiritual gift, we become responsible for the use of it. Jesus makes this clear in the parable of the talents found in Matthew 25:14-19:

> **For the kingdom of heaven is as a man travelling into a far country, who called his own servants, and delivered unto them his goods. And unto one he gave five talents, to another two, and to another one; to every man according to his several ability; and straightway took his journey. Then he that had received the five talents went and traded with the same, and made them other five talents. And likewise he that had received two, he also gained other two. But he that had received one went and dug in the earth, and hid his lord's money. After a long time the lord of those servants cometh, and rekoneth with them.**

In verse 14, Jesus was referring to Himself as the man who travelled into a far country. The far country is earth and the servants represent the body of Christ (Jesus' disciples). Jesus delivered unto them His goods. Goods are a type of spiritual gifts as confirmed in Ephesians 4:7-11:

> **But unto every one of us is given grace according to the measure of the gift of Christ. Wherefore he saith, when he ascended up on high, he led captivity captive, and gave gifts unto men. (Now that he ascended, what is it but that he also descended first into the lower parts of the earth? He that descended is the same also that ascended up far above all heavens, that he might fill all things.) And he gave some, apostles; and some, prophets; and some, evangelists; and some, pastors and teachers.**

Verse 7 tells us that every believer receives a gift of grace. After Jesus ascended, He distributed spiritual gifts unto men. Not every believer will receive one or more of these five-fold ministry offices as we can see by the usage of the word "some." Paul's list of ministry offices here are separate from the list found in 1 Corinthians 12:28. He makes them separate for two reasons:

1. The ministry offices found in Ephesians 4:11 are to perfect and mature believers.

2. The ministry offices found in 1 Corinthians 12:28 are to aid and support the body of Christ.

Believers receive different spiritual gifts (talents and abilities) according to the office(s) they have been called into. We saw this in the parable of the talents as well as in Ephesians 4:8. To some Christians, this might appear like an unequal distribution of spiritual gifts since one servant received five talents, and another two, and another one.

Notice in Matthew 25:15 Jesus said, "to every man according to his several ability." The Greek word for "several" is *idios*, which means pertaining to one's own private or separate self. "Ability" used here in the Greek is *dunamis power*. God's miraculous power is defined here as an ability residing in a person. Greek synonyms for ability are power, strength and work. We can see by the definition of several abilities why Jesus distributes gifts differently. Every Christian has received spiritual gifts according to the miraculous power of God that is working through them separately as an individual. To make this clearer, let's look at some more scriptures.

> **For we dare not make ourselves of the number, or compare ourselves with some that commend themselves: but they measuring themselves by themselves, and comparing themselves among themselves, are not wise. But we will not boast of things without our measure, but according to the measure of the rule which God hath distributed to us, a measure to reach even unto you.**
>
> **2 Corinthians 10:12, 13**
>
> **For I say, through the grace given unto me, to every man that is among you, not to think of himself more**

highly than he ought to think; but to think soberly, according as God hath dealt to every man the measure of faith. For as we have many members in one body, and all members have not the same office.

Romans 12:3, 4

Every believer has been distributed a measure from God. The measure God has given to you is different from what has been given to anyone else in the body of Christ. This is why Paul warns us not to compare ourselves with anyone else in the body of Christ. "Compare" used here means to judge one person with another by way of contrast or resemblance. Paul says you cannot compare one person with another because they are different. Hebrews 12:1 tells us we are to run the race with patience. In track, there are long distance runners, sprinters and hurdlers which are not comparable, since each requires different abilities. Likewise, this is true in the body of Christ. God wants you to run your own race, the one He has prepared for you. Remember that all Christians are running different races but they are running for the same goal: to win in Christ Jesus. We are all to "...press toward the mark for the prize of the high calling of God in Christ Jesus" (Philippians 3:14).

Romans 12:3 tells us not to think of ourselves more highly than we ought but to think soberly. "Soberly" means realistically in the Greek. Paul tells the believers to think realistically about their measure (limited portion) of faith. This limited portion of faith that has been deposited in every believer is different. If you are called to be a teacher in the body of Christ, then your measure (limited portion) will enable you to do just that. But if you do not think realistically about your calling and start moving out and trying to be a pastor, you will find yourself in trouble. Why? Because your limited portion does not include those abilities (strength and power).

Stepping into a position for which you are not equipped will cause you to struggle in your own natural ability, resulting in frustration. It won't work! Spiritual gifts do not come from our own fleshly efforts. These are supernatural gifts given to the body of Christ by a measure of faith which enables the believer to operate through God's ability accomplishing God's objectives. After stepping out and taking responsibility for the spiritual gifts (talents and abilities) that God has entrusted to you, it won't take long to see your limited portion of faith develop and grow.

> **I beseech you therefore, brethren, by the mercies of God, that ye present your bodies a living sacrifice, holy, acceptable unto God, which is your reasonable service. And be not conformed to this world: but be ye transformed by the renewing of your mind, that ye may prove what is that good, and acceptable, and perfect, will of God.**
>
> **Romans 12: l, 2**

"Good" in the Greek means valuable, whereas "acceptable" means well pleasing or fully agreeable. "Perfect" in the Greek means completeness, full maturity or "Christ like. This shows us the progression in our walk with God. Stepping out and using your spiritual gifts (talents and abilities) that God has entrusted to you causes growth. As you step out in obedience to do your work in the ministry, you are able to move from God's good (valuable), to His acceptable (useful and profitable) and to His perfect will, which is the ability to be Christ like. Walking in God's perfect will only come when you take responsibility for using the spiritual gifts (talents and abilities) He has entrusted to you.

For precept must be upon precept, precept upon precept; line upon line, line upon line; here a little and there a little...

Isaiah 28:10

Our Christian walk is progressive. You don't start out at the top. God's perfect will operating in your life comes from being faithful with the little things He gives you to do. Let's go back and look at the end of the parable of talents which confirms this statement.

And so he that had received five talents came and brought other five talents, saying, Lord, thou delivedst unto me five talents: behold, I have gained beside them five talents more. His lord said unto him, well done, thou good and faithful servant: thou hast been faithful over a few things, I will make thee ruler over many things: enter thou into the joy of thy lord. He also that had received two talents came and said, Lord, thou deliveredst unto me two talents: behold, I have gained two other talents beside them. His lord said unto him, well done, good and faithful servant; thou hast been faithful over a few things, I will make thee ruler over many things: enter thou into the joy of thy lord. Then he which had received the one talent came and said, Lord, I

knew thee that thou art an hard man, reaping where thou hast not sown, and gathering where thou hast not strawed: And I was afraid, and went and hid thy talent in the earth: lo, there thou hast that is thine. His lord answered and said unto him, thou wicked and slothful servant, thou knewest that I reap where I sowed not, and gather where I have not strawed: Thou oughtest therefore to have put my money to the exchangers, and then at my coming I should have received mine own with usury. Take therefore the talent from him, and give it unto him which hath ten talents. For unto every one that hath shall be given, and he shall have abundance: but from him that hath not shall be taken away even that which he hath. And cast ye the unprofitable servant into outer darkness: there shall be weeping and gnashing of teeth.

Matthew 25:20-30

In verses 21 and 23 Jesus said, "Well done, thou good and faithful servant: thou hast been faithful over a few things, I will make thee ruler over many things: enter thou into the joy of thy lord." Servants, as discussed earlier, represent Christians. Notice Jesus said His servant was faithful over few things. When you start stepping out in using your spiritual endowments, you are not going to be immediately placed in a teacher's position or on the board. Jesus said, "few" which means small. You start out by cleaning the church, working in the nursery or being faithful at attending the services. Be faithful in whatever God leads you to do!

Study to shew thyself approved unto God, a workman that need not to be ashamed...

2 Timothy 2: 15

Study means to earnestly and diligently make an effort. God expects His servants to start at the bottom and diligently make an effort at being faithful over the few things, which will result in God exalting them.

God is the One who is responsible for exalting us. We are responsible for being faithful with the few things that He has given us to do. God will humble those who elevate themselves. Jesus, in Luke 14:7-11, told His disciples when invited to a wedding not to sit at the head table because someone more distinguished might come along. He told them to sit in the lowest position farthest away from the head table so that the host might say, "...Friend, go up higher...." "For whosoever exalteth himself shall be abased; and he that humbleth himself shall be exalted" (Luke 14:11). These scriptures confirm that if we are faithful in the little things, God will be able to trust us and give us larger responsibilities.

In review we find that there are three parts to a spiritual gift:

1. A God-given ability

2. Service or function

3. Recipient

A spiritual gift is a God-given ability to function effectively in a particular service to benefit a member or members of the body of Christ.

We also found the recipient of a spiritual gift becomes qualified and responsible in using God's ability, strength and power. It is God's responsibility to qualify believers. The believer's responsibility is to accept his spiritual gifts (talents and abilities) and step out and use them, which results in glorifying the Father God.

Herein is my Father glorified, that ye bear much fruit; so shall ye be my disciples.

John 15:8

God's will is for you to use the spiritual gifts (talents and abilities) which have been entrusted to you. We saw in the parable of the talents that Jesus trusted His servants to use what they had been given. Make a decision to accept your responsibility, step out, and use the spiritual gifts He has entrusted to you. The ability to bear fruit in your life comes from using the spiritual gifts the Father God has given to you.

For we are his workmanship, created in Christ Jesus unto good works, which God hath before ordained that we should walk in them.

Ephesians 2:10

Upon accepting Jesus Christ as your personal Lord and Savior you no longer live for yourself but rather for Jesus Christ and the Father God. Before the foundations of the earth, God had a purpose and an individual plan He created just for you. The Word tells us to choose now this day whom you'll serve. Make a decision to walk in God's prearranged plan for your life.

I believe the following chapters will enlighten your spiritual understanding of how God's spiritual gifts work through believers, accomplishing His will in their lives.

3

CONCERNING SPIRITUAL GIFTS

Now concerning spiritual *gifts*, brethren, I would not have you ignorant.

1 Corinthians 12: 1

The word "gifts" here in the King James Version, is in italics which means it was not in the original Greek translation. "Spiritual" is *pneumatikos* in the Greek which literally means spiritualities. The definition of spiritualities is grace made manifest or grace made specific. A spiritual gift is a grace (a free gift from God) made manifest (displayed by supernatural power working through the believer). The use of "spiritualities" in this verse refers to all spiritual gifts in general and does not refer to any specific list.

Paul is telling believers not to be ignorant of spiritual gifts. We can see the importance of this, because if you don't know and understand spiritual gifts you won't use them or earnestly desire them.

... desire spiritual gifts...

1 Corinthians 14:1

The word "spiritual" used here, in the Greek, is the same word as in 1 Corinthians 12: 1. Spiritual gifts are important to ALL believers because they are God-given talents and abilities. The purpose of each spiritual gift found in the New Testament is to work through the believer to accomplish God's will on earth (Philippians 2:13). Paul gives us information regarding spiritual gifts:

> **Now there are diversities of gifts, but the same Spirit. And there are differences of administrations, but the same Lord. And there are diversities of operations, but it is the same God which worketh all in all.**

1 Corinthians 12:4-6

In these verses, Paul gives us a complete picture of how ministry is accomplished in the body of Christ. In verse 4, he tells us there are diversities of gifts. "Gifts" used here, in the Greek, is a reference to numerous endowments available to believers by the operation of the Holy Spirit. The Holy Spirit is in charge of the spiritual gifts. Verse 5 tells us there are differences of administrations. "Administrations" is diakonia in the Greek meaning offices. There are different offices as listed in Ephesians 4:11 and 1 Corinthians 12:28. Notice Paul tells us, "...but the same Lord..."; Jesus Christ is Lord and head over the offices.

Verse 6 tells us there are "diversities of operations." "Operations" in the Greek is energeo meaning God's active and operative power.

Our English word "energy" is derived from *energeo*. Paul is stating in these verses that it is the same God whose energizing power works through all of the gifts in all of the offices of Jesus Christ.

The spiritual gifts that you operate in are governed by the ministry office(s) you are called into. For example, someone called by God to be a pastor would be equipped with several gifts, one of which is teaching. We can see in Ephesians 4:11 that there is no semicolon between "pastor" and "teacher" unlike the other offices. Paul links these two offices together. Therefore, we can assume that a pastor must have the gift of teaching. You cannot be a pastor without being able to teach, as further substantiated in 1 Peter 5:2 where Peter exhorts pastors in their duties.

...Feed the flock of God which is among you...

There are two parts to the Greek word "feed" used here:

1. To act as a <u>SHEPHERD</u> (keep sheep) to watch over believers to protect them.

2. To <u>NOURISH,</u> as in the special function of being able to provide believers with spiritual food.

Do you see the necessity of knowing and understanding spiritual gifts? In order to be effective in serving God, you need to know what spiritual gifts (endowments) have been entrusted to you. This will help you find your office(s) in the body of Christ. For example, if you are called to be a counselor, it is imperative that you have wisdom along with discernment working through you. If you do not have those abilities working through you, it's time to re-evaluate your calling. God equips you with everything needed to fulfill your calling in the body of Christ.

The ministry that God requires to come forth from the body of Christ is not from our own fleshly efforts, talents or abilities, but from the spiritual gifts that God has imparted to us by the Holy Spirit. These are supernatural gifts that work through believers by God's miraculous power. We are not to look at these gifts as if they are natural talents and abilities.

Now we can see why it is important that we "...desire spiritual gifts." (1 Corinthians 14:1). The place where God has put you in the body of Christ is determined by the spiritual gifts that He has entrusted to you.

> **But now hath God set the members every one of them in the body, as it hath pleased him.**
> **1 Corinthians 12:18**

It is God, and not the believer, who chooses his place in the body of Christ. This is one of the major problems Christians face today. Everyone except God is putting Christians in their place in the body. There might be a need for teachers in a particular church so they start filling positions by availability and not gifting, which results in frustrated Christians since it is not their calling. They lose their joy and find themselves struggling and striving to teach in their own fleshly effort, which will not work. God requires the individual's ministry to come from the talents and abilities that are given by Him.

Every believer has been given grace (spiritual endowments) according to the measure of the gift of Christ.

> **But unto every one of us is given grace (spiritual endowments) according to the measure of the gift (office) of Christ.**
>
> **Ephesians 4:7 (explanation mine)**

"Gift" used here in the Greek, refers to the office(s) in which we are called to stand. Every believer has a divinely ordained ministry office in the body of Christ and no one can take his place. Each believer has received spiritual graces relating to the ministry office(s) in which he stands. Your gifts and callings cannot be fulfilled by someone else.

We are now going to look at each list of spiritual gifts found in the New Testament. The objective of this chapter is to give an overall view of all spiritual gifts found in the Bible. The main focus of this book is an in-depth study of the gifts of grace (commonly known as motivation gifts) found in Romans 12:6-8. However, in order for you to understand the gifts of grace and their purpose for the body of Christ, it first becomes necessary for you to know the other lists of spiritual gifts, thereby preventing any confusion or misunderstandings.

Let's look at our first list of spiritual gifts found in 1 Corinthians 12:7-11:

PHANEROSIS: MANIFESTATIONS OF THE HOLY SPIRIT

> **But the manifestation of the Spirit is given to every man to profit withal. For to one is given by the Spirit**

the word of wisdom; to another the word of knowledge by the same Spirit; to another faith by the
same Spirit; to another the gifts of healing by the
same Spirit; to another the working of miracles; to
another prophecy; to another discerning of spirits;
to another divers kinds of tongues; to another the
interpretation of tongues: But all these worketh
that one and the self-same Spirit, dividing to every
man severally as he will.

Verse 7 informs us these gifts are manifestations of the Holy
Spirit. "Manifestations" in the Greek means open to sight or
visible. The Holy Spirit becomes openly visible for a brief period
of time to manifest one of the following gifts found in verses 8-10.
Manifestations of the Holy Spirit are available to every believer as
acknowledged in verses 7 and 11 but notice it is as the Holy Spirit
directs. These spiritual gifts are used by God as a brief expression
of the Holy Spirit to profit a member or members of the body of
Christ.

Let's look at the Greek definitions of these spiritual gifts:

1. WORD OF WISDOM:

The word of wisdom is a supernatural revelation by the
Spirit of God concerning the divine purpose in the mind
and will of God for the future. This is only a fragmented
part of God's wisdom. Agabus gave a word of wisdom
by the Spirit regarding a future famine (Acts 11:28).

2. WORD OF KNOWLEDGE:

The word of knowledge is a supernatural revelation by the Holy Spirit to enable understanding of God's truth regarding people, places and things. This knowledge is either past or present and is not obtained by intellect but by the operation of the Holy Spirit working through believers. Jesus told the Samaritan woman at the well about her five husbands and the man she was living with (John 4:18).

3. FAITH:

Every believer has been given the measure of faith (Romans 12:3). However, the gift of faith is a supernatural gift of a special kind of faith. This gift of faith is directed by the Holy Spirit and activates God's power in a believer's life resulting in the working of a miracle. The woman with the issue of blood was healed because of the gift of faith working within her (Luke 8:48).

4. GIFTS OF HEALING:

The gifts of healing are supernatural cures of infirmities and diseases. These are divinely imparted gifts that result in a cure. Gifts of healing directed by the Holy Spirit operate through one believer to another. The gift of faith works the miracle in the believer who receives it, whereas the gifts of healing operate through a believer toward another person. There are a variety of gifts of healing as we can see by the plurality of the word "gifts". Peter and John had a gift of healing work through them when they lifted the lame man to his feet, for immediately his feet and ankle bones received strength (Acts 3:7).

5. WORKING OF MIRACLES:

Working of miracles is a supernatural intervention in the ordinary course of nature. It is brief, perceptible and enacted by the force of the Holy Spirit. Jesus performed the working of a miracle at the marriage in Cana of Galilee when He turned the water into wine (John 2:9). Another working of a miracle was the parting of the Red Sea (Exodus 14:21).

6. PROPHECY:

This gift of prophecy should not be confused with the ministry gift of a prophet or the gift of grace of prophecy. The characteristics of these gifts are the same but they are three separate and distinct gifts. These three gifts are fully defined in the chapter of this book on prophecy. The gift of prophecy is a supernatural revelation into the mind and counsel of God.

The manifestations of the Holy Spirit are fragmented (brief and perceptible) pieces of revelation. Agabus prophesied to Paul regarding the perils that awaited him in Jerusalem (Acts 21:11).

7. DISCERNING OF SPIRITS:

The discerning of spirits gives insight into the spirit world to reveal both good and evil. This is a supernatural revelation into the spiritual realm. We can see a good example of this in Acts 7:55,56 when Stephen was being stoned to death. Stephen "...looked up steadfastly into heaven, and saw the glory of God, and Jesus standing on the right hand of God, and said, Behold I see the heavens opened, and the Son of man standing on the right hand of God." Stephen saw into the spiritual realm. Another example of the discerning of spirits is found in Acts 16:16-19 where it tells about a woman possessed with a spirit of divination who was following Paul. It took Paul several days before he operated in the discerning of spirits and cast the demon out of her.

8. DIVERSE KINDS OF TONGUES:

The word "diverse" is in italics in the King James Version, which tells us the word was added by the translator. Literally this scripture should read to another kinds of tongues. "Kinds," in the Greek, means diversity, so it is acceptable to say diverse kinds of tongues. "Tongues" defined in the Greek means a language that is unacquired or unlearned. In Acts 2:4, we see that on the day of Pentecost, all believers were filled with the Holy Ghost and spoke with other tongues as the Spirit gave them utterance. Once you receive the baptism of the Holy Spirit and speak in tongues, you are free to use it any time you will or desire. The gift of tongues is different in that it operates as the **Spirit** wills and is for the edifying of the church. Paul explains this in 1 Corinthians 14:5, 6: "I would that ye all spake with tongues, but rather that ye prophesied: for greater is he that prophesieth than he that speaketh with tongues, except he interpret, that the church may receive edifying. Now, brethren, if I come unto you speaking with tongues, what shall I profit you, except I shall speak to you either by revelation, or by knowledge, or by prophesying, or by doctrine?" Essentially, Paul states that prophecy is equal to tongues and interpretation. Without the interpretation of tongues there is no understanding and therefore, no profit to the body of Christ. It is important that the person who comes forth with tongues be able to interpret, thus edifying the hearers.

Wherefore tongues are for a sign, not to them that believe, but to them that believe not: but prophesying serveth not for them that believe not, but for them which believe.

1 Corinthians 14:22

Paul tells us the gift of tongues, when spoken in a church, becomes a sign to unbelievers that the unlearned language is from God. Prophecy, on the other hand, is for believers, not unbelievers.

9. INTERPRETATION OF TONGUES:

The gift of interpretation of tongues depends upon and is in response to the operation of the gift of tongues. The purpose of the interpretation is to inform the hearer's intellect so he can be edified. The interpretation of tongues is the understanding spoken forth by the individual who has been given the revelation by the Holy Spirit.

THESE NINE MANIFESTATIONS OF THE HOLY SPIRIT ARE DIVIDED AS FOLLOWS:

- **Three are revelation gifts (that reveal information):**

  Word of wisdom
  Word of knowledge
  Discerning of spirits

- **Three are power gifts (that work in or for believers):**

  Gift of faith
  Working of miracles
  Gifts of healing

- **Three are utterance, or illuminating gifts (that edify, exhort and comfort):**

  Prophecy
  Tongues
  Interpretation of tongues

DIAKONIA: ADMINISTRATIONS (MINISTRIES)

The second list of spiritual gifts is found in 1 Corinthians 12:28. These are administrations or ministry offices.

And God hath set some in the church, first apostles, secondarily prophets, thirdly teachers, after that miracles, then gifts of healings, helps, governments, diversities of tongues.

1 Corinthians 12:28

This is a list of some of the ministry offices God has placed in His Church. We saw earlier in 1 Corinthians 12:18 that God places members in the body as it pleases HIM. God has placed an order to these offices, as the scripture reads first apostles, secondarily prophets, thirdly teachers, etc. The usage of the word "some" before the list of gifts tells us not all believers will operate in these particular offices. However, there is a place or office that each believer will be called to stand in that might not necessarily be out in the forefront, such as church janitor, Sunday school teacher, choir member, intercessor, etc. We are still a team and all members are required to play. No one is benched on God's team. We need to remember that we are all equally important. There are no star attractions, for God is no respecter of persons. For example, you might be called to work in the nursery. This position might not look important to you, but it is to God. Jesus said, "...Suffer the little children to come unto me...." (Mark 10:14). The word also tells us, "Train up a child in the way he should go...." (Proverbs 22:6). Children are important to God for they are a heritage from Him. God is equally concerned on Sunday morning with the pastor feeding His flock as with the nursery worker taking care of His children.

DEFINITION OF THE ADMINISTRATION GIFTS

1. APOSTLES:

A full explanation will follow in the section on Ministry Gifts later in this chapter.

2. PROPHETS:

A full explanation will follow in the section on Ministry Gifts later in this chapter.

3. TEACHERS:

The word "teachers" used here in the Greek is defined as teachers of the truth, and/or instructor or doctor.

Sanctify them through thy truth: thy word is truth.
John 17:17

Jesus Christ is our example of the world's greatest teacher. John tells us, "In the beginning was the Word and the Word was God..." (John 1:1). Jesus Christ cannot be separated from His Word since they are one and the same. The teaching ministry is a divine calling from God with supernatural endowments that include the ability to expound and transmit revelation knowledge from God's Word.

A teacher does not teach in his own natural ability or by his own desire or inclination. The ministry of teaching is fulfilled by the supernatural power of the Holy Spirit working through the believer. Again, these administration gifts are given by God's placement of the believer in the body as it pleases Him.

4. MIRACLES:

The Greek word for miracles is *dunamis* meaning God's miraculous power. This power is an inherent ability of a supernatural origin and character displayed through mighty works. A miracle is an interruption in the ordinary course of nature by the Holy Spirit. One example of the working of miracles in the Old Testament is Joshua in the Valley of Ajalon when he commanded the sun and moon to stand still (Joshua 10:12, 13). The magnitude of this miracle is overwhelming since the entire universe, including the earth, stopped moving. Peter performed a miracle in the town of Joppa when he raised Tabitha (known as Dorcas) from the dead (Acts 9:40).

5. GIFTS OF HEALING:

"Gifts" used here, in the Greek, is defined as God's endowments upon believers by the operation of the Holy Spirit. The Greek word for healings is *lama* in the Greek meaning the cure. These are divinely imparted gifts that result in a cure. Gifts of healing operate through one believer to another or to the unsaved. There are a variety of gifts of healing as we can see by the plurality of these words. Numerous examples of gifts of healings are given in the Bible. Jesus operated in the gifts of healings at the pool of Bethesda when He told the man with an infirmity to rise and take up his bed and walk (John 5:1-9). Peter operated in the gifts of healings when he went to Lydia and said to the man with palsy, "...Jesus Christ maketh thee whole: arise, and make thy bed" (Acts 9:32-35).

6. HELPS:

The definition of the Greek word for helps is relief and/ or participate by support. We could say the ministry of helps is a helper of the saints. The ministry of helps is one of the administration gifts set up by God in the local church to render assistance. This particular administration gift covers a lot of ministry offices because of the many areas of support needed in the church. It is noteworthy that administration gifts are connected with service in a local church.

Let's look at some biblical examples of the ministry of helps.

And it came to pass afterward, that he went throughout every city and village, preaching and shewing the glad tidings of the Kingdom of God: and the twelve were with him, and certain women, which had been healed of evil spirits and infirmities, Mary called Magdalene, out of whom went

seven devils, and Joanna the wife of Chuza Herod's steward, and Susanna, and many others, which ministered unto him of their substance.

Luke 8:1-3

The word substance used here, in the Greek, means property or possessions. The word "ministered" in the Greek is *diakoneo* defined as supplying the necessities of life. Notice these women ministered to Jesus Christ of their substance. When you serve and/or minister in the body of Christ, it is important to remember you do it as unto the Lord Jesus Christ. "And whatsoever ye do, do it heartily, as to the Lord, and not unto men; knowing that of the Lord ye shall receive the reward of the inheritance: for ye serve the Lord Christ" (Colossians 3:23, 24). The women in Luke 8 were motivated by the gift of grace of giving and serving. Their gifts of grace motivated them toward the office of ministry of helps. The obedience of Mary, Joanna, Susanna and other women operating in the ministry of helps freed Jesus and His disciples to give themselves continually to prayer and to the ministry of the Word (Acts 6:4).

Lydia, Paul's first European convert in Philippi, showed hospitality to Paul, along with Luke, Silas and other brethren.

And they went out of the prison, and entered into the house of Lydia: and when they had seen the brethren, they comforted them, and departed.

Acts 16:40

Lydia had the gift of grace of serving that motivated her toward her office in the body of Christ. Servers are fulfilled when they are meeting the needs of those around them. Lydia probably did not realize that her desire to bless Paul and his colleagues came from God's "efficient energy" working from within her gift of grace.

The ministry of helps aids or supports any area in the local church. For example:

CHURCH JANITORS promote the smooth operation of a church.

CHOIR MEMBERS aid in leading the corporate body of believers into worship.

USHERS assist the pastor by keeping order in the church, taking up offerings, and ministering communion.

NURSERY ATTENDANTS support believers by taking care of God's heritage (His children (Psalm 127:3) so parents can assemble together in corporate fellowship and receive teaching.

CHURCH SECRETARIES attend to the pastor's needs to promote an efficiently operating church.

MUSICIANS aid in leading the corporate body of believers into worship.

SOUND ENGINEERS oversee the sound board and record messages of the pastor, guest speakers, and special music.

WOMEN'S MINISTRIES aid and support the pastor and the church. They organize church socials, prayer chains, and usually offer a weekly Bible study. This group not only helps the pastor and the church in meeting needs that arise, but it also adds a strong nucleus to the church.

These are only a few of the ministry offices that aid or support the local church. I chose these offices because of their lack of recognition in the body of Christ. The body of Christ has recognized that deacons, elders and church board members are in the ministry of helps, but the offices listed above are generally not recognized as ministries. Nevertheless, every office is a divine calling of God that has been originated by Him to supply all the needs of the local church. Let's start appreciating every ministry as a God-ordained office given to meet the needs of the church.

7. GOVERNMENTS:

The Greek word for governments is *kubemesis* in the Greek defined as pilotage or directorship, meaning those acting as guides in the local church. Titus had the administration gift of governments so Paul left him in Crete to organize the church and ordain elders (Titus 1:5). Peter displayed the administration gift of governments when he took leadership as the principal preacher on the day of Pentecost (Acts 2:14). He also took charge of administering discipline in Acts 5:3, 4 when he sentenced Ananias and Sapphira to death. Some examples of those with the gift of governments include:

> EDUCATIONAL DIRECTORS oversee Sunday school teachers and their yearly curricula. They promote the smooth operation of educational programs in the church.

BUS MINISTERS head the bus ministry for their church. They promote the smooth operation of bus transportation for Sunday school, church and other related functions.

ASSOCIATE PASTORS head a particular area of ministry in the church bringing aid and support to the pastor and the church. Associate pastors inlcude youth pastor; larger churches may have an education pastor (for home Bible studies); music pastor (leads choir for regular and special functions); visitation pastor (visits the sick and elderly who can't attend church); and evangelism pastor (heads up the outreach ministries).

8. DIVERSITIES OF TONGUES:

"Diversities" is defined as diverse tongues in the original Greek. The word "tongues" in the Greek is *glossa* meaning "a language that is naturally unacquired or unlearned."

The phrase "kinds of tongues" found in 1 Corinthians 12:10 and "diversities of tongues" found in 1 Corinthians 12:28 have the same Greek definition. However, the context in which the words are used is entirely different. There are four points that support this statement.

* The usage of the word "some" in 1 Corinthians 12:28 tells us not all Christians will have the ministry office of diversities of tongues. Yet Paul tells us in 1 Corinthians 12:7, 8 that every man can operate in the manifestations of the Holy Spirit as the Spirit wills. This is not a contradiction in the Word of God but rather a statement concerning two distinctly different gifts.

53

* 1 Corinthians 12:28 tells us God is in charge of the ministry of diversities of tongues, whereas verse 11 tells us the Holy Spirit is in charge of diverse kinds of tongues.

* The manifestations of the Holy Spirit are for a brief period of time, as previously discussed in this chapter. The Holy Spirit openly becomes visible (working through a believer) for a brief period of time to manifest one of His gifts. These gifts (1 Corinthians 12:8-10) are distributed temporarily by the Holy Spirit who divides them as He wills. The administrations (1 Corinthians 12:28) are set permanently in the church. These are permanent gifts set in the church by God until Jesus comes back for His bride.

* Paul links the interpretation of tongues in 1 Corinthians 12:10 with divers kinds of tongues, whereas in verse 28, we find diversities of tongues with no mention of an interpretation. The reason for this is because tongues and interpretation have not been set in the church as a permanent ministry office. This is in no way referring to your personal prayer language (Acts 2:4); that is entirely a separate operation. We are talking specifically in regards to diverse kinds of tongues (1 Corinthians 12:10) and diversities of tongues (1 Corinthians 12:28). Paul asks the question, "Do all have the same office in the body of Christ? "Certainly not, since he just told us in verse 28 that some are set in each of these offices.

Verse 31 is a continuation of the thought carried through verses 28 to 30. Paul's ending comment in verse 31 to covet earnestly the best gifts, is an exhortation encouraging believers to desire gifts (1 Corinthians 12:8-10) that would enhance their ministry office in the body of Christ. For example, if a believer is called into the area of counseling, they need to believe God for the three revelation gifts (word of wisdom, word of knowledge, and discerning of spirits). Why? Because those gifts are the best gifts for that ministry. Without the revelation gifts working through them, it would be impossible for them to be effective counselors.

In conclusion, we find diversities of tongues and diverse kinds of tongues play two separate roles in the body of Christ. Therefore, what is diversities of tongues used for? Paul is referring to intercessors who have been set as an office of authority in the church. God sets intercessors in the church as a permanent ministry office.

And I [Lord God] sought for a man among them, that should make up the hedge, and stand in the gap before me for the land, that I should not destroy it; but I found none.

Ezekiel 22:30 (explanation mine)

God sets intercessors in the church and they represent a separate office found in the administration gift of diversities of tongues. It is a gift that is desperately needed in the body of Christ. God searches for intercessors who will sacrificially stand in the gap and make up the hedge for the body of Christ.

The Greek word for "intercessor" means to make a petition or intercede on behalf of another in the intercessory work of the Holy

Spirit. Notice the definition states that intercession is the work of the Holy Spirit, referring to interceding in the Spirit in other tongues. Paul refers to the ministry office as diversities of tongues since tongues is an effective way of intercession. The other effective method of intercession is to pray with understanding in your natural language (1 Corinthians 14:15).

> **Likewise the Spirit also helpeth our infirmities: for we know not what we should pray for as we ought: but the Spirit itself maketh intercession for us with groanings which cannot be uttered. And he that searcheth the hearts knoweth what is the mind of the Spirit, because he maketh intercession for the saints according to the will of God.**
>
> **Romans 8:26, 27**

These scriptures inform believers that the Holy Spirit works with them, taking hold together in intercession. The Holy Spirit helps believers to pray in the spirit (tongues) when they don't know what to pray for or how to pray. The Holy Spirit makes intercession for believers because He knows what to pray according to the will of God.

KATARTISMOS: ADMINISTRATIONS (MINISTRY OFFICES)

The third list is also a list of administrations (ministry offices) commonly called the five-fold ministry by the body of Christ. The purpose of this group of offices is to prepare the body of Christ by equipping them. They are called *katartismos* because these gifts are for the "perfecting" of the saints and the word perfecting in the Greek is *katartismos*. The ministry offices are a direct extension of Jesus Christ himself.

> **Wherefore he saith, when he ascended up on high, he led captivity captive, and gave gifts unto men. And he gave some, apostles; and some, prophets; and some, evangelists; and some, pastors and teachers; For the perfecting of the saints, for the work of the ministry, for the edifying of the body of Christ.**
> **Ephesians 4:8,11, 12**

Verse 8 tells us Jesus gave "gifts" which in the Greek is *doma* meaning ministry gifts. As we studied in chapter 1, "perfecting" means to fully prepare. These gifts prepare believers for their work in the ministry. The last part of verse 12 tells us these gifts are for the edifying of the body. Edifying is the act of promoting spiritual growth. These ministry offices promote spiritual growth in believers causing unity to come to the body. Individuals anointed with these special ministry offices are a blessing to the entire body of Christ. Every believer will not necessarily be given one of these five-fold ministry offices as we can see by the usage of the word "some" before each office. However, these five offices should be available through some to develop each believer.

MINISTRY GIFT DEFINITIONS

Ephesians 4:11 is a partial list of ministry offices. The list in 1 Corinthians 12:28 was previously discussed in this chapter.

1. APOSTLES:

The Greek definition for "apostle" means to be a delegate or an ambassador to the Gospel; officially a commissioner of Christ operating with miraculous powers; a messenger who has been sent. *W.E. Vine's Expository Dictionary* states that the twelve disciples chosen by the Lord for special training were called apostles. Let's examine a scripture that defines the characteristics of an apostle: "And he (Jesus Christ) ordained twelve, that they should be with him, and that he might send them for to preach, and to have power to heal sicknesses, and to cast out devils" Mark 3:14, 15 (explanation mine).

It is apparent that the essential characteristic or qualification of an apostle is a divine call, commissioned by Jesus Christ. The second characteristic Jesus mentioned is that the apostles should be with him.

> **...and ye shall be witnesses unto me [Jesus Christ]
> both in Jerusalem, and in all Judea, and in Samaria,
> and unto the uttermost parts of the earth.**
>
> **Acts 1:8 (explanation mine)**

> **Beginning from the baptism of John, unto that
> same day that he was taken up from us, must one be
> ordained to be a witness with us of his resurrection.**
>
> **Acts 1:22**

Jesus' apostles were a group of men appointed to be with Him. The primary function of the apostles, as we see in Acts 1:22, was to be witnesses of Jesus Christ. It also tells us the time span this witnessing would take place (from the baptism of John until Jesus' ascension), which involved years of obtaining knowledge combined with experience and intensive training, for the apostles' recognized office was to be witnesses to the resurrection.

The third characteristic that Jesus required of His apostles was their ability to preach. Jesus' apostles were not only required to bear witness of His resurrection, but they were also to remind the people of Jesus' words by guiding them to the truth. The church is built on the foundation of the apostles and prophets:

> **And that he [Jesus Christ] might reconcile both unto God in one body by the cross, having slain the enmity thereby: And came and preached peace to you which were afar off, and to them that were nigh. For through him we both have access by one Spirit unto the Father. Now therefore ye are no more strangers and foreigners, but fellow citizens with the saints, and of the household of God; and are built upon the foundation of the apostles and prophets, Jesus Christ himself being the chief corner stone.**
>
> **Ephesians 2:16-20 (emphasis mine)**

The foundation is Jesus Christ; therefore, the apostles preached Jesus Christ, the author and finisher (developer) of their faith.

> **For other foundation can no man lay than that is laid, which is Jesus Christ.**
>
> **1 Corinthians 3: 11**

The last characteristic of an apostle is the authority to heal and to exorcise devils.

And by the hands of the apostles were many signs and wonders wrought among the people.

Acts 5:12

Acts continues to tell us that these miracles were healings and the casting out of unclean spirits. The apostles' purpose was to be with Him (Jesus Christ), to preach the foundation message, and to have authority to heal and cast out demons.

And the apostles gathered themselves together unto Jesus, and told him all things, both what they had done, and what they had taught.

Mark 6:30

Mark used the word "apostles" here in this scripture referring to the successful return of the twelve from a mission of preaching and healing. This was a miniature assignment in preparation for their future task "...Unto the uttermost parts of the earth" (Acts: 1:8).

Are there apostles today? Some of you might be wondering how there can be present day apostles when Jesus "...ordained twelve that they should be with him..." (Mark 3:14). Obviously there are no Christians today who can meet Jesus' requirement of being with Him; therefore, how can there be any present day apostles? Paul states he is an apostle in Galatians 1:1:

Paul, an apostle, (not of men, neither by men, but by Jesus Christ, and God the Father, who raised him from the dead).

Notice Paul (not one of the original twelve disciples) said he is an apostle, not by men but by Jesus Christ. The original twelve apostles were set apart for a special purpose. Paul lets us know Jesus continues today to appoint apostles in the church. In 1 Timothy 2:7 Paul testifies: "Whereunto I am ordained a preacher, and an apostle, (I speak the truth in Christ, and lie not;)..." It is noteworthy that Paul links his ordination of apostleship to preaching and speaking the truth. These are two of the characteristics of an apostle. The last characteristic of an apostle are signs and wonders confirming God's Word being preached.

> **That I should be the minister of Jesus Christ to the Gentiles, ministering the gospel of God, that the offering up of the Gentiles might be acceptable, being sanctified by the Holy Ghost. I have therefore where of I may glory through Jesus Christ in those things which pertain to God. For I will not dare to speak of any of those things which Christ hath not wrought by me, to make the Gentiles obedient, by word and deed, through mighty signs and wonders, by the power of the Spirit of God; so that from Jerusalem, and round about unto Illyricum, I have fully preached the gospel of Christ.**
>
> **Romans 15:16-19**

Paul makes it clear that Jesus Christ had sent him forth to preach the Gospel through sanctification by the Holy Ghost. In verse 19, Paul's preaching of Jesus Christ was confirmed through mighty signs and wonders, by the power of the Holy Spirit.

We can see that Paul's ministry was not hindered in any way by not being part of the original twelve apostles. Paul gave us more revelation knowledge concerning the Church Age than any other apostle of the church.

2. PROPHETS:

A prophet is defined as a foreteller or seer inspired to speak forth and proclaim a divine message on the mind and counsel of God. Another definition for prophet is a message coming from God that has been secretly communicated. "The Word of the Lord came" is a statement that was used literally hundreds of times in the Old Testament, leaving no real indication whether it came by way of the thought process, through a vision, audibly, or in some other way.

> **Beforetime in Israel, when a man went to inquire of God, thus he spake, Come, and let us go to the seer: for he that is now called a Prophet was beforetime called a Seer.**
>
> **I Samuel 9:9**

Prophets were called seers because God would let them see a fragmented portion of what was secret.

> **Surely the Lord GOD will do nothing, but he revealeth his secret unto his servants the prophets. The lion hath roared, who will not fear? The Lord GOD hath spoken who can but prophesy?**
>
> **Amos 3:7, 8**

How does God reveal His secrets? Verse 8 tells us He reveals His secrets by speaking unto the prophets. The messages of the Old Testament prophets were largely centered on the proclamation of the divine purposes of salvation and God's glory to be accomplished in the future. In Isaiah 53:1-8, the prophet received a message from God regarding His salvation plan. Isaiah had received revelation regarding the suffering and death of Jesus.

Joel was another prophet who received a fragmented glimpse into the future. The outpouring of the Holy Spirit described in Joel 2:28 was a prophetic utterance. Joel was the tool used by God for a divine revelation which had significance far beyond his understanding.

> **And it shall come to pass afterward, that I will pour out my spirit upon all flesh; and your sons and your daughters shall prophesy, your old men shall dream dreams, your young men shall see visions.**

This revelation was definitely a secret that God had opened to Joel who delivered the message in a prophetic utterance.

Prophets in the New Testament preached on the fundamentals of Christianity and future events regarding the mind of the Spirit.

> **And when he was come unto us, he took Paul's girdle, and bound his own hands and feet, and said Thus saith the Holy Ghost, So shall the Jews at Jerusalem bind the man that owneth this girdle, and shall deliver him into the hands of the Gentiles.**
>
> **Acts 21:11**

Agabus the prophet gave Paul a warning of future events regarding what was going to happen to him when he entered Jerusalem.

3. EVANGELISTS:

Evangelists are messengers of good news; they are preachers of the Gospel of Jesus Christ. The word "evangelist" is found three times in the New Testament: Ephesians 4: 11, Acts 21:8, 2 Timothy 4:5.

Philip is our example of an evangelist in the New Testament. Notice both of Philip's messages to Samaria and to the Eunuch were to preach Jesus Christ. What is the supernatural equipment that comes with the evangelist's gift?

> **Then Philip went down to the city of Samaria, and preached Christ unto them.**
>
> **Acts 8:5**

> **Then Philip opened his mouth, and began at the same scripture, and preached unto him Jesus.**
>
> **Acts 8:35**

> **And the people with one accord gave heed unto those things which Philip spake, hearing and seeing the miracles which he did. For unclean spirits, crying with loud voice, came out of many that were possessed with them: and many taken with palsies, and that were lame, were healed. And there was great joy in that city.**
>
> **Acts 8:6-8**

The supernatural "gifts of healing" and "miracles" are some of the spiritual equipment necessary for an evangelist. Healings and miracles followed the preaching of Jesus Christ by Philip. Miracles and healings draw a crowd but only believing in the Word of God brings salvation.

4. PASTORS AND TEACHERS:

The word "pastors" is used only once in the King James translation of the New Testament and is linked to the word "teachers" as we saw in Ephesians 4:. 11. Therefore, pastors are required to be teachers. This is confirmed in Acts 20:28:

> **Take heed therefore unto yourselves, and to all the flock, over the which the Holy Ghost hath made you overseeers, to feed the church of God, which he hath purchased with his own blood.**

As we can see by this scripture, pastors are to oversee (guide and watch over) as well as feed their flock. The spiritual care of God's children has been entrusted to the pastors. Father God expects pastors to regularly feed their flock the Word of God.

> **The elders which are among you I exhort, who am also an elder, and a witness of the sufferings of Christ, and also a partaker of the glory that shall be revealed: Feed the flock of God which is among you, taking the oversight thereof, not by constraint, but willingly; not for filthy lucre, but of a ready mind; Neither as being lords over God's heritage, but being examples to the flock. And when the Chief Shepherd shall appear, ye shall receive a crown of glory that fadeth not away.**
>
> **1 Peter 5: 1-4**

Jesus Christ is the Chief Shepherd of all of God's sheep, whereas pastors are the under-shepherds answering directly to the Lord Jesus Christ.

Peter uses the word "elders" in reference to pastors, of which he says he is one. Peter's instructions give us a clear picture of the pastors' responsibility to be overseers of the flock of God. Included in his instructions to the pastors, Peter warns them not to lord over their flock. Pastors must realize they are a direct extension of the Lord and as such are accountable for leading and guiding their flock as Jesus Christ would.

Tending a flock consists of acts of discipline, restoration, material assistance for individuals, counseling and ruling. You cannot separate caring for the flock from the feeding. Pastors who teach their flock promote spiritual growth resulting in numerical growth in their disciples.

I am the Good Shepherd: the Good Shepherd giveth his life for his sheep.

John 10:11

Notice Jesus said He is the Good Shepherd. "Good" in this scripture means appealing in the Greek. Appealing means attractive, captivating, magnetic, likeable, lovely and fascinating. It is imperative that pastors be imitators of Jesus Christ and likewise be appealing. When presenting our Lord, pastors as well as individual believers should remember that if we present it correctly, it would be hard for listeners not to accept Jesus Christ as their personal Lord and Savior.

CHARISMAS: GIFTS OF GRACE (MOTIVATIONAL GIFTS)

I BESEECH you therefore, brethren, by the mercies of God, that ye pre sent your bodies a living sacrifice, holy, acceptable unto God, which is your reasonable service. And be not conformed to this world: but be ye transformed by the renewing of your mind, that ye may prove what is that good, and acceptable, and perfect, will of God. For I say, through the grace given unto me, to every man that is among you, not to think of himself more highly than he ought to think; but to think soberly, according as God hath dealt to every man the measure of faith. For as we have many members in one body, and all members have not the same office: So we, being many, are one body in Christ, and every one members one of another. Having then gifts differing according to the grace that is given to us, whether prophecy, let us prophesy according to the proportion of faith; or ministry, let us wait on our ministering: or he that teacheth, on teaching; or he that exhorteth, on exhortation: he that giveth, let him do it with simplicity; he that ruleth, with diligence; he that sheweth mercy, with cheerfulness.

Romans 12:1-8

In 1 Corinthians 12:6, we find there are "diversities of opera-tions." The word "operations" in the Greek is defined as energizing.

The gifts of grace listed in Romans 12:6-8 are the unique energizings of the Holy Spirit working through the believer causing the desire and the power to concentrate on a particular aspect of a spiritual concern. The gift of grace given to each believer is unique because it works and operates differently in each believer's life. The study of the gifts of grace is important because every Christian views other Christians and circumstances through their gift of grace. For example, Christians with the gift of grace of ruling look at things through the eyes of an administrator, whereas Christians with the gift of grace of teaching look at things through the eyes of a teacher.

In Romans 12:6, the word "gifts," in the Greek means a gift involving grace on the part of God as the donor. These endowments are given to believers by the operation of the Holy Spirit. The gifts of grace are commonly known as the motivational gifts because they carry the power to motivate the believer. The Holy Spirit works these gifts through believers motivating them toward their ministry offices (1 Corinthians 12:28 and Ephesians 4:11). These spiritual gifts are the primary focus of this book. The other three lists of spiritual gifts have been mentioned to educate the reader.

Paul tells us in Romans 12:1 that we are required by God to offer ourselves as a living sacrifice. That is the first step believers should take upon receiving Jesus Christ as their personal Lord and Savior. The second step is in verse 2, "...be not conformed to this world: but be ye transformed by the renewing of your mind." Transforming your mind can only come one way, by the Word of God. Let the Word of God change your thinking to His thinking. Why? Paul continues by telling us you can then prove what God's good, acceptable, and perfect will is concerning your life. This shows us the progressive nature of our walk with the Father God. We start out walking in the good will of God, growing into His acceptable will and graduating to His perfect will. Ephesians 5:1 tells us what God's perfect will is:

Be ye therefore followers of God as dear children.

The word translated "followers" is defined as "imitators" in the Greek. We are told here to follow or imitate God. In Galatians 2:20, Paul tells us he is crucified with Christ and no longer will he live in the flesh but Christ lives in and through him. He allowed the Greater One to live in him by letting the Word of God have first place in his life. The essence of the gifts of grace in Romans 12 is that the believer must realize that he has been created for God's pleasure and no longer lives as an island unto himself.

The gifts of grace are given by God to help believers accomplish His perfect will in their lives. Romans 12:3,6 tells us every believer has received a gift of grace. "For I say, through the grace given unto me, to every man that is among you,..." and "Having then gifts differing according to the grace that is given to us." Paul uses the word "grace" in a singular tense supporting the truth that each believer receives one gift of grace. The gift of grace given to each believer is unique because it works and operates differently in each believer's life. This unique grace of God will cause believers to be motivated in the direction they should go, producing unique effects in their life. We can see these unique effects displayed through Paul's life in Galatians 2:7-9.

But contrariwise, when they saw that the gospel of the uncircumcision was committed unto me, as the gospel of the circumcision was unto Peter; (For he that wrought effectually in Peter to the apostleship of the circumcision, the same was mighty in me toward the Gentiles:) And when James, Cephas, and John, who seemed to be pillars, perceived the grace that was given unto me, they gave to me and Barnabas the right hands of fellowship; that we should go unto the heathen, and they unto the circumcision.

James, Cephas, and John were having problems understanding Paul's motivation toward the Gentiles. The body of Christ faces the same stumbling block today. God produces unique effects in the believer's life and all of us are different. Paul states in verse 8 that God was motivating him toward the Gentiles, whereas Peter was being motivated toward the Jews. Notice Paul said it was the same God who was working in both of them, yet they were being motivated in opposite directions. This is an excellent example of unique effects working in the believers. Verse 9 says James, Cephas and John finally "...perceived the grace that was given unto me...."

"Perceived" means to come to know and fully understand. It took awhile before the disciples were fully persuaded that Paul's ministry was from God. Why? Paul's gift of grace was motivating him in a different direction than his colleagues and was producing a unique effect. The body of Christ needs to mature in this area by realizing God motivates each believer in a direction that will produce a unique effect. If you put two people in charge of the same project it would produce two unique effects. Paul said that after they perceived his ministry was from God, they gave him the right hand of fellowship. "Fellowship" means communication. In the body of Christ, we often don't understand why people are motivated in a certain direction and this results in broken communication and division. The body of Christ needs to perceive that believers are being motivated by God and not by their own fleshly efforts or desires.

Reviewing Galatians 2:8, notice the word "wrought." In the Greek, it is *energeo*, meaning God's operative and active power. As we studied earlier our word "energy" is derived from this word. *Energeo* is God's energizing power which is active and operative in believers' lives through their gift of grace.

"Wrought" means to put forth power, operative and active availing to the work of the Lord. Paul said the energizing power of God was working through both he and Peter, but it was motivating them in opposite directions. There are no carbon copies in the body of Christ. Every believer is an original when he presents his body as a living sacrifice and allows God to produce unique effects in his life.

The gifts of grace are given by God to activate believers' faith and cause them to move toward their ministry offices in the body of Christ. The question arises, will two people with the same gift of grace produce the same results? No, the same gift of grace will work differently in each believer's life producing unique effects.

Paul and John the Baptist were both motivated by the gift of grace of prophecy, yet they produced unique effects. John was called as a prophet sent to prepare the way for Jesus Christ. His ministry was directed toward the Jews, whereas Paul's ministry was toward the Gentiles. Paul was called as an apostle, prophet, evangelist, preacher and teacher. Even though both men had the same gift of grace working through them, they were motivated toward different ministry offices in the body of Christ.

The gift of grace effectually working in you should be producing unique effects. Your unique effects should differ from anyone else in the body of Christ. The gift of grace that God has entrusted to you will motivate you toward a ministry (1 Corinthians 12:28 and Ephesians 4:11). The gift of grace is the motivation to minister in the body of Christ.

Paul and John the Baptist are excellent examples of how God works differently in each believer. Here are two men of God who had spiritual gifts working through them producing unique effects. As ambassadors of Christ, they represented His life differently. The chart on the following page shows how John the Baptist's and Paul's lives were parallel, yet they produced unique effects.

JOHN THE BAPTIST AND PAUL — AMBASSADORS OF CHRIST

JOHN THE BAPTIST
JEW
gift of grace of prophecy
motivated John toward his ministry in the body of Christ
EVANGELIST PROPHET TEACHER
Produced unique effects

72

PREACHED AND TAUGHT

THE JEWS

PAUL

ADOPTED JEW

gift of grace of prophecy

motivated Paul toward his ministry in the body of Christ

EVANGELIST PROPHET TEACHER

APOSTLE PASTOR

Produced unique effects

PREACHED AND TAUGHT

THE GENTILES

It is imperative the body of Christ realize that God works through each believer differently. Paul tells us in 1 Corinthians 12:6, "...it is the same God which worketh all in all."

BELIEVER

gift of grace

motivates them toward their ministry

in the body of Christ

The gift of grace is expressed through their office

and/or ministry

PRODUCING UNIQUE EFFECTS

CREATED TO SERVE

Mankind was created for God's pleasure. We were made in His image with the purpose to serve Him. With this purpose in mind, we need to look at God's supernatural gifts working in believers motivating them to minister as servants.

The body of Christ needs to perceive that the ministries that come from God's people are not derived from their fleshly efforts, natural talents or abilities, but rather are spiritual gifts given by God. God empowers believers to exercise their gifts, talents, and abilities efficiently to benefit a member or members of the body of Christ.

A common misunderstanding is about how many gifts of grace each believer receives. Each believer receives ONE gift of grace at the time of their spiritual birth. We know this from Paul's comment in Romans 12:4 "...all members have not the same office." Office here is singular, not plural. The believer receives one gift of grace but is required to operate in all seven of the gifts of grace. The believer's gift of grace influences his operation of the other gifts of grace. For example, if you have the gift of grace of mercy and are operating in prophecy, you will come from the direction of the merciful side of God. Another example is the person with the gift of grace of exhortation operating in teaching will be motivated to stimulate the truths that he is revealing. The believer's main emphasis in his gift of grace doesn't change when he operates in the other six gifts of grace. He is still motivated by one gift of grace.

There are four lists of illustrations on the following pages. The first three illustrate Jesus Christ, Peter and Paul operating in all seven gifts of grace. Jesus Christ is the only one who was equally motivated in all of the gifts of grace. The last list shows us through the Word of God that we are required and accountable to operate in all seven gifts of grace.

ILLUSTRATIONS OF THE GIFTS OF GRACE
IN THE LIFE OF JESUS CHRIST

PROPHECY: (TO CORRECT) MARK 11:15-17

And they came to Jerusalem: and Jesus went into the temple, and began to cast out them that sold and bought in the temple, and overthrew the tables of the moneychangers, and the seats of them that sold doves; and would not suffer that any man should carry any vessel through the temple. And he taught, saying unto them, Is it not written, My house shall be called of all nations the house of prayer? but ye have made it a den of thieves.

Jesus corrected the moneychangers and the other men misusing the house of God.

SERVING: (TO ATTEND TO PRACTICAL NEEDS) MARK 6:34-38, 41, 42

And Jesus, when he came out, saw much people, and was moved with compassion toward them, because they were as sheep not having a shepherd: and he began to teach them many things. And when the day was now far spent, his disciples came unto him, and said, This is a desert place, and now the time is far passed: Send them away, that they may go into the country round about, and into the villages, and buy themselves bread: for they have nothing to eat. He answered and said unto them, Give ye them to

> eat. And they say unto him, Shall we go and buy two hundred penny worth of bread, and give them to eat? he saith unto them, How many loaves have ye? go and see. And when they knew, they say, Five, and two fishes. And when he had taken the five loaves and two fishes, he looked up to heaven, and blessed, and brake the loaves, and gave them to his disciples to set before them; and the two fishes divided he among them all. And they did all eat, and were filled.

This account in Mark shows Jesus meeting the practical needs of 5,000 men, and also all of the women and children.

TEACHING: (TO REVEAL TRUTH) MATTHEW 4:23

> And Jesus went about Galilee, teaching in their synagogues, and preaching the gospel of the kingdom, and healing all manner of sickness and all manner of disease among the people.

Jesus taught the true principles of the scripture.

EXHORTATION: (TO STIMULATE FAITH) MARK 10:17-22

> And when he was gone forth into the way, there came one running, and kneeled to him, and asked him, Good Master, what shall I do that I may inherit eternal life? And Jesus said unto him, Why callest thou me good? There is none good but one, that is, God. Thou knowest the commandments, Do not commit adultery, Do not kill, Do not steal, Do not bear false witness, Defraud not, Honour

thy father and mother. And he answered and said unto him, Master, all these have I observed from my youth. Then Jesus beholding him loved him, and said unto him, One thing thou lackest: go thy way, sell whatsoever thou hast, and give to the poor, and thou shalt have treasure in heaven: and come, take up the cross, and follow me. And he was sad at that saying, and went away grieved: for he had great possessions.

Jesus dealt with the rich man by discerning his deepest need and exhorting him with steps of action which would have resulted in eternal treasures.

GIVING: (TO SPEND ONE'S LIFE WITH AND FOR OTHERS) JOHN 10:17, 18; MATTHEW 20:28

Therefore doth my Father love me, because I lay down my life, that I might take it again. No man taketh it from me, but I lay it down of myself. I have power to lay it down, and I have power to take it again. This commandment have I received of my Father.

Even as the Son of man came not to be ministered unto, but to minister, and to give his life a ransom for many.

The greatest gift the world will ever see was when the Father God gave His only begotten son Jesus, who laid down His life freely for mankind, and gave Himself a ransom for many.

RULING: (TO ORGANIZE) MARK 6:39-41

> **And he commanded them to make all sit down by companies upon the green grass. And they sat down in ranks, by hundreds, and by fifties.**

Jesus commanded the multitudes to sit down by companies and then gave His disciples instructions on how to feed the people.

MERCY: (TO SHOW OR HAVE COMPASSION THAT LEADS TO HELP) Matthew 20:30, 32-34

> **And, behold, two blind men sitting by the way side, when they heard that Jesus passed by, cried out, saying, Have mercy on us, O Lord, thou Son of David. And Jesus stood still, and called them, and said, What will ye that I shall do unto you? They say unto him, Lord, that our eyes may be opened. So Jesus had compassion on them, and touched their eyes: and immediately their eyes received sight, and they followed him.**

Jesus was moved by compassion that resulted in these two blind men receiving their sight. Mercy is God's unmerited favor that always gives you the answer.

ILLUSTRATIONS OF THE GIFTS OF GRACE OPERATING IN PETER'S LIFE

PROPHECY: (TO CORRECT) ACTS 5:3, 4, 8, 9

> **But Peter said, Ananias, why hath Satan filled thine heart to lie to the Holy Ghost, and to keep back**

part of the price of the land? While it remained, was it not thine own? and after it was sold, was it not in thine own power? why hast thou conceived this thing in thine heart? thou hast not lied unto men, but unto God. And Peter answered unto her, Tell me whether ye sold the land for so much? And she said, Yea, for so much. Then Peter said unto her, How is it that ye have agreed together to tempt the Spirit of the Lord? Behold, the feet of them which have buried thy husband are at the door, and shall carry thee out.

Peter was operating in the gift of grace of prophecy. He perceived, defined and corrected the evil.

SERVING: (TO MEET PRACTICAL NEEDS) ACTS 9:38-42

And forasmuch as Lydda was nigh to Joppa, and the disciples had heard that Peter was there, they sent unto him two men, desiring him that he would not delay to come to them. Then Peter arose and went with them. When he was come, they brought him into the upper chamber: and all the widows stood by him weeping, and shewing the coats and garments which Dorcas made, while she was with them. But Peter put them all forth, and kneeled down, and prayed; and turning him to the body said, Tabitha, arise. And she opened her eyes: and when she saw Peter, she sat up. And he gave her his hand, and lifted her up, and when he had called the saints

and widows, presented her alive. And it was known throughout all Joppa; and many believed in the Lord.

Peter became Jesus' arm extended to a group of widows in their time of need. Dorcas had truly spent her life for others. She died in the middle of her ministry, but Peter, having become a servant just like his Teacher, raised her from the dead.

TEACHING: (TO REVEAL TRUTH) 1 PETER 3:1-5

Likewise, ye wives, be in subjection to your husbands; that, if any obey not the word, they also may without the word be won by the conversation of the wives; while they behold your chaste conversation coupled with fear. Whose adorning let it not be that outward adorning of plaiting the hair, and of wearing of gold, or of putting on of apparel; But let it be the hidden man of the heart, in that which is not corruptible, even the ornament of a meek and quiet spirit, which is in the sight of God of great price. For after this manner in the old time the holy women also, who trusted in God, adorned themselves, being in subjection unto their own husbands.

Peter reveals biblical truths concerning the relationship between husbands and wives.

EXHORTATION: (TO STIMULATE FAITH) ACTS 2:40, 41

And with many other words did he testify and exhort, saying, Save yourselves from this untoward generation. Then they that gladly received his word

were baptized: and the same day there were added unto them about three thousand souls.

Peter's exhortation had a unique effect in which 3,000 souls were added to the Kingdom of God. For further reading on Peter's exhortation, read Acts 2 concerning the day of Pentecost.

RULING: (TO ORGANIZE) 1 PETER 5:1-3

The elders which are among you I exhort, who am also an elder, and a witness of the sufferings of Christ, and also a partaker of the glory that shall be revealed: Feed the flock of God which is among you, taking the oversight thereof, not by constraint, but willingly; not for filthy lucre, but of a ready mind; Neither as being lords over God's heritage, but being examples to the flock.

Notice Peter says, "I exhort" the reason being his gift of grace was exhortation. Your gift of grace will motivate you in a certain direction even when operating in the other gifts of grace. Peter was exhorting the pastors to organize the church of God. He tells them they are responsible for teaching as well as overseeing, but ruling is done with love not power.

GIVING: (TO SPEND ONE'S LIFE WITH OTHERS) MATTHEW 10:1,2

And when he had called unto him his twelve disciples, he gave them power against unclean spirits, to cast them out, and to heal all manner of sickness and all manner of disease. Now the names of the

twelve apostles are these; the first, Simon, who is called Peter.

Peter's acceptance of the call of God in his life to become an apostle and disciple reveals his heart's motive to give his life for the Master's use. His decision meant a willingness to spend his life with and for others.

MERCY: (TO SHOW (OR HAVE) COMPASSION THAT LEADS TO HELP) ACTS 3:2, 6, 7

And a certain man lame from his mother's womb was carried, whom they laid daily at the gate of the temple which is called Beautiful, to ask alms of them that entered into the temple; Then Peter said, Silver and gold have I none; but such as I have give I thee: In the name of Jesus Christ of Nazareth rise up and walk. And he took him by the right hand, and lifted him up: and immediately his feet and ankle bones received strength.

Peter, as an ambassador of Christ, went about doing good and was moved by compassion that always led to help.

ILLUSTRATIONS OF THE GIFTS
OF GRACE OPERATING IN PAUL'S LIFE

PROPHECY: (TO CORRECT) GALATIANS 2:11-14

But when Peter was come to Antioch, I withstood him to the face, because he was to be blamed. For before that certain came from James, he did eat with

the Gentiles: but when they were come, he withdrew and separated himself, fearing them which were of the circumcision. And the other Jews dissembled likewise with him; insomuch that Barnabas also was carried away with their dissimulation. But when I saw that they walked not uprightly according to the truth of the Gospel, I said unto Peter before them all, If thou, being a Jew, livest after the manner Gentiles, and not as do the Jews, why compellest thou the Gentiles to live as do the Jews?

Paul abhorred and defined evil and did it in a direct, frank conversation with Peter. The person with the gift of grace of prophecy is concerned for the program of God. Paul's gift of grace is prophecy and he operated in all seven gifts from the direction of prophecy.

TEACHING: (TO REVEAL TRUTH) HEBREWS 5:12

For when for the time ye ought to be teachers, ye have need that one teach you again which be the first principles of the oracles of God; and are become such as have need of milk, and not of strong meat.

We can see throughout the New Testament that Paul reveals more of the Word of God to us than any other person in the Bible.

SERVING: (TO MEET PRACTICAL NEEDS) 1 CORINTHIANS 16:15, 16

I beseech you, brethren, (ye know the house of Stephanas, that it is the first fruits of Achaia, and that they have addicted themselves to the ministry

of the saints), That ye submit yourselves into such,
and to everyone that helpeth with us, and laboureth.

Paul uses the word "ministry" which is *diakonia* in the Greek (the same Greek word in Roman 12:7 for ministry) meaning serving. It is interesting that the word "serving" in Latin means to trouble one's self. Paul encourages believers to trouble themselves by laboring and/or serving the body of Christ.

EXHORTATION: (TO STIMULATE FATH) HEBREWS 10:25

Not forsaking the assembling of ourselves together,
as the manner of some is; but exhorting one another:
and so much the more, as ye see the day approaching.

Paul exhorted Christians to commit themselves to a body of believers and become faithful in their attendance.

GIVING: (TO SPEND ONE'S LIFE WITH OTHERS) 2 CORINTHIANS 8:1-5

Moreover, brethren, we do you to wit of the grace
of God bestowed on the churches of Macedonia;
How that in a great trial of affliction the abun-
dance of their joy and their deep poverty abounded
unto riches of their liberality. For to their power,
I bear records, yea, and beyond their power they
were willing of themselves; Praying us with much
entreaty that we would receive the gift, and take
upon us the fellowship of the ministering to the
saints. And this they did, not as we hoped, but first

gave their own selves to the Lord, and unto us by the will of God.

Paul had learned the principles of sowing and reaping. he knew once the believers learned to apply this principle to their lives they would never be the same. He spent his whole Christian life giving of himself, his time and his money to the Kingdom of God. This scripture shows him exhorting others to apply this essential principle to their lives.

RULING: (TO ORGANIZE) 1 TIMOTHY 3:4

One that ruleth well his own house, having his children in subjection with all gravity;

Paul tells us another essential principle for believers involved in a church. God holds them responsible for having their house in order before moving out in their ministry.

MERCY: (TO SHOW (OR HAVE) COMPASSION THAT LEADS TO HELP) PHILIPPIANS 2:1, 2

If there be therefore any consolation in Christ, if any comfort of love, if any fellowship of the Spirit, if any bowels and mercies, Fulfill ye my joy, that ye be likeminded, having the same love, being of one accord, of one mind.

Paul's letters to the New Testament church show his concern for the body of Christ. The desire of his heart was to educate believers thus preventing them from being deceived by Satan or themselves.

Paul exemplifies a godly man whose compassion led to the help of numerous believers.

BIBLICAL INSTRUCTIONS REQUIRING CHRISTIANS TO OPERATE IN THE GIFTS OF GRACE

PROPHECY:

> **Follow after charity, and desire spiritual gifts, but rather that ye may prophesy.**
>
> **1 Corinthians 14:1**

TEACHING:

> **Let the word of Christ dwell in you richly in all wisdom; teaching and admonishing one another in psalms and hymns and spiritual songs, singing with grace in your hearts to the Lord.**
>
> **Colossians 3:16**

MINISTRY (SERVING):

> **For God is not unrighteous to forget your work and labour of love, which ye have shewed toward his name, in that ye have ministered to the saints and do minister. And we desire that every one of you do shew the same diligence to the full assurance of hope unto the end:**
>
> **Hebrews 6:10, 11**

EXHORTATION:

But exhort one another daily, while it is called today; lest any of you be hardened through the deceitfulness of sin.

Hebrews 3:13

GIVING:

Every man according as he purposeth in his heart, so let him give not grudgingly, or of necessity: for God loveth a cheerful giver.

2 Corinthians 9:7

RULING (ORGANIZING):

And let the peace of God rule in your hearts, to which also ye are called in one body; and be ye thankful.

Colossians 3:15

MERCY:

Put on therefore, as the elect of God, holy and beloved, bowels of mercies, kindness, humbleness of mind, meekness, longsuffering.

Colossians 3:12

The purpose of the gifts of grace is to bring success and unity into the body of Christ as each individual operates in his special gift of grace. Understanding your primary gift of grace will free you to grow, develop, and express yourself as God has created you. It will help you recognize your importance to God and the body of Christ, and appreciate your brothers and sisters in Christ the way God has created them. Being a good steward of your time is also affected by your gift of grace since you will be able to focus your efforts on what God has called you to do, thereby saving time.

This study is <u>not for the purpose of labeling others; however it is for self-analysis</u> which is as a catalyst for growth in ourselves and understanding others.

Each believer's strength lies in his gift of grace. You will see yourself in all seven gifts because Jesus Christ operated in all seven gifts and you are called to be imitators of Him. However, the key to finding your gift of grace is the joy and satisfaction received from operating in it (Isaiah 55:10, 11). Your gift of grace will bring joy that is unspeakable and full of glory.

SPIRITUAL GIFTS

CHARISMAS	PHANEROSIS	DIAKONIA	KATARTISMOS
Gifts of Grace	Manifestations of the Spirit	Ministry Gifts	Five -Fold Ministriy Gifts
Romans 12:6-8	1 Cor. 12:7-11	1 Cor. 12:5-28	Ephesians 4:8-12

PURPOSE:

To motivate the believer toward his ministry in the body of Christ where God has placed him (1 Cor. 12:18)	A brief expression of the Holy Spirit to profit a member in the body of Christ.	To show how God has set up His ministries in His church.	For the maturing of the saints through spiritual growth.

RECIPIENT:

"for I say through the grace given unto me, to EVERY MAN that is among you..." Romans 12:3	"But the manifestation of the Spirit is given to EVERY MAN to profit withal." 1 Cor. 12:7	And God has set SOME in the church..." 1 Cor. 12:28 (every believer has been placed in at least one of the following offices listed below)	"And he gave SOME apostles; and SOME prophets; and SOME evangelists; and SOME pastors and teachers..." Ephesians 4:11

GIFTS:

Prophecy	Word of Wisdom	Apostles	Apostles
Serving	Word of Knowledge	Prophets	Prophets
Teaching		Teachers	Evangelists
Exhortation	Faith	Miracles	Pastors
Giving	Healing	Gifts of Healing	Teachers
Ruling	Miracles	Helps	
Mercy	Discerning of Spirits	Governments	
	Kinds of Tongues	Diversities of Tongues	
	Interpreation of tongues		

The Gift Of Grace Of Prophecy

Having then gifts differing according to the grace that is given to us, whether prophecy, let us prophesy according to the proportion of faith.

Romans 12:6

"Prophecy" used here, in the Greek, is *propheteia* defined as an inspired speaker; one who speaks forth the mind and counsel of God. As discussed earlier, believers must think <u>realistically about their measure </u>(limited portion) of faith. Notice this verse says, "let us prophesy according to the proportion of faith." The limited portion of faith given with the gift of grace of prophesy enables the believer to operate through God's ability, thereby accomplishing His goals. A believer stepping out beyond his portion of faith will find himself working through his own fleshly efforts.

There is a lot of confusion between the following three spiritual gifts:

1. **PROPHET**: Ephesians 4:11; 1 Corinthians 12:28

2. **PROPHECY:** 1 Corinthians 12:10

3. **GIFT OF GRACE OF PROPHECY:** Romans 12:6

Let's look at the Greek definitions of these three spiritual gifts, clarifying each gift's purpose within the body of Christ.

1. A prophet as mentioned in Ephesians 4:11, is a person who has a call of God on his life. He is sent forth by God as an inspired speaker to establish spiritual truths. This gift is a way of life. One of the definitions of prophet is an occupation. We can see in 1 Corinthians 12:28 that God has set this gift as an office of authority in the church.

    And God has set some in the church, first apostles, secondarily prophets.

2. The manifestation of the Holy Spirit's gift of prophecy is found in 1 Corinthians 12: 10. This gift is a brief expression of the Holy Spirit manifesting himself through a believer. It is for a specified time, given to edify, exhort, and comfort a member or members of the body of Christ.

    But he that prophesieth speaketh unto men to edification, and exhortation, and comfort.
    1 Corinthians 14:3

The manifestation of the Holy Spirit's gift of prophecy does not affect your lifestyle because it is for a brief period of time.

3. The <u>gift of grace of prophecy</u> described in Romans 12:6 motivates the believer toward his ministry office in the body of Christ. This spiritual gift is a motivation or a cause to function, and operates in the believer from his spiritual birth.

The prophet, the gift of prophecy, and the gift of grace of prophecy are three different gifts, as we have seen in their definitions. Although in Scripture, we find that the same basic principles, guidelines and knowledge apply to all three of these spiritual gifts. The basic principles for prophecy flow through all three of these spiritual gifts, even though they are exercised differently.

Let's look further into the definition of prophecy. Prophecy proclaims the truth and reveals what God knows to be the inner heart motives or actions of people, situations or groups. Another way of describing prophecy is that it corrects or instructs. Now we are going to let the Word of God define and give us insight into the gift of grace of prophecy.

> **(Beforetime in Israel, when a man went to inquire of God, thus he spake, Come, and let us go to the seer: for he that is now called a Prophet was beforetime called a Seer.)**
>
> **1 Samuel 9:9**

We can see here that a prophet is a seer, defined as one who sees things that are hidden. People with the gift of grace of prophecy have a divine ability to see that which is in secret.

> **But if all prophesy, and there come in one that believeth not, or one unlearned, he is convinced of all, he is judged of all: And thus are the secrets of his heart made manifest; and so falling down on his face he will worship God, and report that God is in you of a truth.**
>
> **1 Corinthians 14:24, 25**

The word "judged" here in the Greek is *anakrino* meaning scrutinize, discern and examine. "Judged" used in this scripture refers to the ability to probe the conscience of one who is not right with God. Verse 25 tells us the secrets of such a person's heart are made manifest. The person with the gift of grace of prophecy has the ability to probe the conscience and manifest secrets that are in the hearts of people, groups and churches. The ability of one with the gift of grace of prophecy to reveal hidden secrets of the heart helps the unbeliever realize that God is working through His people. We can see this by the end of verse 25, where it tells us the unbeliever will fall down and worship God because of the hidden revelation that has been prophesied.

> **But the natural man receiveth not the things of the Spirit of God: for they are foolishness unto him: neither can he know them, because they are spiritually discerned.**
>
> **1 Corinthians 2:14**

Prophecy is spiritual discernment with the ability to reveal inner heart motives by divine inspiration of the Holy Spirit working through the believer.

Let's further examine 1 Corinthians 14:24. Verse 24 tells us when a person comes in who does not believe in Jesus Christ or is unlearned, he is convinced. "Unlearned" in the Greek, is defined as spiritual ignorance. A person with the gift of grace of prophecy is intolerant of doubt, unbelief and spiritual ignorance. He has the ability to spiritually discern in these areas, bringing out into the open what is wrong .

As we said earlier, another way of defining prophecy is to correct (constructive correction).

> **For they verily for a few days chastened us after their own pleasure; but he for our profit, that we might be partakers of his holiness. Now no chastening for the present seemeth to be joyous, but grievous: nevertheless afterward it yieldeth the peaceable fruit of righteousness unto them which are exercised thereby.**
>
> **Hebrews 12:10-11**

This passage tells us it's hard to receive correction (chastening). "Chasteneth" is *paideuo* in the Greek, meaning to instruct, teach, correct, educate and learn. Prophecy is defined as correction and instruction regarding God's mind and thoughts. Our promise from God if we yield to His chastisement and correction is to receive the peaceable fruit of righteousness.

The gift of grace of prophecy is one of the most misunderstood gifts in the body of Christ. This does not alter the fact that it is a gift desperately needed in the body of Christ. Prophecy points us directly back to God and enables us to see Him as the God who continues to confront sin.

> **Before I formed thee in the belly I knew thee; and before thou earnest forth out of the womb I sanctified thee, and I ordained thee a prophet unto the nations... Then the Lord put forth his hand, and touched my mouth. And the Lord said unto me, behold, I have put my words in thy mouth. See, I have this day set thee over the nations and over the kingdoms, to root out, and to pull down and to destroy and to throw down to build, and to plant.**
>
> **Jeremiah 1:5, 9, 10**

HEBREW DEFINITIONS

ROOT OUT: to pluck out by the roots

PULL DOWN: break and tear down

DESTROY: to make undone

THROW DOWN: to utterly break down in pieces (ruin)

BUILD: to make, repair, set up surely

PLANT: to fasten securely

This passage paints a clear picture of constructive correction whereby after the sin is rectified the person is edified, exhorted and comforted by the planting of God's Word. The first thing to note in these scriptures is that God ordained Jeremiah to be a prophet. Spiritual gifts are not operated by fleshly efforts or callings but are God ordained. God tells us the benefits of prophecy are to root out, pull down, destroy, throw down, build and plant. The person with the gift of grace of prophecy has the ability to correct and instruct as directed by the Holy Spirit. God starts out by telling us of needed corrections in order for Him to be able to instruct (build and plant). Prophecy has been given to probe our inner heart motives and actions so they can be revealed and corrected. After the corrections are made, God can plant His Word by fastening it securely to our hearts.

> **But he that prophesieth speaketh unto men to edification, and exhortation, and comfort.**
>
> **1 Corinthians 14:3**

We can see three benefits of prophecy in this scripture: edification, exhortation, and comfort. Prophecy is used to help develop the body of Christ to maturity, as we can see in the Greek definitions of these words.

EDIFICATION: architecture, structure, building

EXHORTATION: comfort, consolation, entreaty

COMFORT: consolation

> **And ye have forgotten the exhortation which speaketh unto you as unto children, My son, despise not thou the chastening (correction) of the Lord, nor faint when thou are rebuked of him: For whom the Lord loveth he chasteneth (corrects), and scourgeth every son who he receiveth. If ye endure chastening (correction), God dealeth with you as with sons; for what son is he whom the father chasteneth not?**

> **But if ye be without chastisement, whereof all are partakers, then are ye bastards, and not sons. Furthermore we have had fathers of our flesh which corrected us, and we gave them reverence: shall we not much rather be in subjection unto the Father of spirits, and live?**
>
> **Hebrews 12:5-9, explanation mine**

We can see that exhortation, comfort, and correction are all tied together in the gift of prophecy. The importance of chastening or correction is revealed in these scriptures, for it is a part of the education and training of a child of God. Receiving correction is a prerequisite of God's instruction (building and planting). Prophecy is a benefit and help to the body of Christ. Prophecy always edifies, exhorts, and comforts. You can judge prophecy, for if it is critical and does not give any comfort or help (answer), then it is not from God. God does correct, but He will always follow through with edification, exhortation, and steps of action leading to an answer.

Now we are going to look at biblical examples of two individuals with the gift of grace of prophecy.

JOHN THE BAPTIST

John the Baptist was called by God as a prophet:

> **But what went ye out for to see? A prophet? Yea, I say unto you, and much more than a prophet. This is he, of whom it is written, Behold, I send my messenger before thy face, which shall prepare thy way before thee. For I say unto you, Among those that are born**

of women there is not a greater prophet than John the Baptist: but he that is least in the kingdom of God is greater than he.

Luke 7:26-28

Being a prophet of God was a way of life for John. He was not only a prophet but also motivated by the gift of grace of prophecy. Let's look at the characteristics of the gift of grace of prophecy demonstrated through the life of John the Baptist.

And he came into all the country about Jordan, preaching the baptism of repentance for the remission of sins; As it is written in the book of the words of Isaiah the prophet, saying, The voice of one crying in the wilderness, Prepare ye the way of the Lord, make his paths straight. Every valley shall be filled, and every mountain and hill shall be brought low; and the crooked shall be made straight, and the rough ways shall be made smooth; and all flesh shall see the salvation of God. Then said he to the multitude that came forth to be baptized of him, O generation of vipers, who hath warned you to flee from the wrath to come? Bring forth therefore fruits worthy of repentance, and begin not to say within yourselves, We have Abraham to our father: for I say unto you, That God is able of these stones to raise up children unto Abraham. And now also the axe is laid unto the root of the trees: every tree therefore which bringeth not forth good fruit is hewn down, and cast into the fire. And the people asked him,

saying, What shall we do then? He answereth and saith unto them, He that hath two coats, let him impart to him that hath none; and he that hath meat, let him do likewise. Then came also publicans to be baptized, and said unto him, Master, what shall we do? And he said unto them, Exact no more than that which is appointed you. And the soldiers likewise demanded of him, saying, And what shall we do? And he said unto them, Do violence to no man, neither accuse any falsely; and be content with your wages. And as the people were in expectation, and all men mused in their hearts of John, whether he were the Christ, or not; John answered, saying unto them all, I indeed baptize you with water; but one mightier than I cometh, the latchet of whose shoes I am not worthy to unloose: he shall baptize you with the Holy Ghost and with fire: Whose fan is in his hand, and he will thoroughly purge his floor, and will gather the wheat into his garner; but the chaff he will burn with fire unquenchable. And many other things in his exhortation preached he unto the people. But Herod the tetrarch, being reproved by him for Herodias his brother Philip's wife, and for all the evils which Herod had done, added yet this above all, that he shut up John in prison.

Luke 3:3-20

Verse 3 tells us John preached the baptism of repentance for the remission of sins. The person with the gift of grace of prophecy has the ability to identify, define and hate sin (evil). In verse 4, it tells us John the Baptist was a voice crying in the wilderness. John's deep need to express his message verbally is another characteristic of a person with the gift of grace of prophecy. This person feels grief and personal identification with the sins of people and expresses that grief verbally. Expressing their message verbally does not mean that those with the gift of grace of prophecy are talkative, but rather their speech is usually important and direct.

John the Baptist knew that Jesus was coming yet this message had not been revealed to the Jews yet. The person with the gift of grace of prophecy has the ability to spiritually discern that which is in secret. We can also see John's spiritual discernment in verses 16 and 17, when the people were wondering in their hearts if he was the Christ. He tells them he is not but was sent to prepare the way for a man who would come whose sandals he was not worthy to tie.

Verses 7, 8, and 19 show John the Baptist probing the conscience of the people around him by confronting their sins. People with the gift of grace of prophecy have the ability to probe the conscience of those around them and manifest secrets that are in their hearts, as directed by the Holy Spirit. We can see John the Baptist's intolerance of spiritual ignorance and unbelief in verse 9.

People with the gift of grace of prophecy are direct, frank, and honest in their conversation. John the Baptist had no problem with being direct as we can see in verse 7 where he called the multitudes a generation of vipers. We can also see John's honesty and frankness in Matthew 11:2, 3:

**Now when John had heard in the prison the works
of Christ, he sent two of his disciples, and said unto
him, Art thou he that should come, or do we look
for another?**

John sent two of his disciples to Jesus asking if He was Christ
the Messiah or if they should look for another? John had baptized
Jesus in the beginning of His ministry. He had seen the heavens
open and the Spirit descend on Jesus as a dove. John had also heard
the Father God say, "This is My Son in whom I am well pleased."
Why then would John ask Jesus if He was the Messiah? This question was important to John since his gift of grace of prophecy had
validated Jesus' authority. The person with the gift of grace of prophecy has a dependence on scriptural truth to validate authority. John
the Baptist's concern stemmed from reports of Jesus eating with the
tax collectors. Notice Jesus addressed the question without taking
offense.

**...Go and shew John again those things which ye
do hear and see: The blind receive their sight, and
the lame walk, the lepers are cleansed, and the deaf
hear, the dead are raised up, and the poor have the
gospel preached to them. And blessed is he, whosoever shall not be offended in me.**

Matthew 11:4-6

Jesus gave John scriptures from the Old Testament (Isaiah 35:5,
6) to validate His authority. John had heard of Jesus eating with
publicans and socializing with people of low moral character. John's
gift of grace of prophecy working through him caused him to hate

evil so he could not understand why Jesus would socialize with evil-doers. Jesus said, "They that are whole have no need of the physician, but they that are sick: I came not to call the righteous, but sinners to repentance" (Mark 2:17). Jesus ended His message to John in Matthew 11:6 by telling him not to be offended (stumble) by Him.

DEBORAH:

Let's look at another person with the gift of grace of prophecy in the Bible. Her name is Deborah and her story is found in Judges 4:1, 4-9.

> **And the children of Israel again did evil in the sight of the Lord, when Ehud was dead... And Deborah, a prophetess, the wife of Lapidoth, she judged Israel at that time. And she dwelt under the palm tree of Deborah between Ramah and Bethel in mount Ephraim: and the children of Israel came up to her for judgement. And she sent and called Barak the son of Abinoam out of Kedesh-naphtali, and said unto him, Hath not the Lord God of Israel commanded, saying, Go and draw toward mount Tabor, and take with thee ten thousand men of the children of Naphtali and of the children of Zebulun? And I will draw unto thee to the river Kishon Sisera, the captain of Jabin's army, with his chariots and his multitude; and I will deliver him into thine hand. And Barak said unto her, If thou wilt go with me, then I will go: but if thou wilt not go with me, then I will not go. And she said, I will surely go with thee;**

**notwithstanding the journey that thou takest shall
not be for thine honour; for the Lord shall sell Sisera
into the hand of a woman. And Deborah arose, and
went with Barak to Kedesh.**

There are several characteristics in Deborah's life that correlate
with the life of John the Baptist. Verse 1 tells us the children of Israel
AGAIN did evil in the sight of their Lord. We saw in Luke 3:7, 8
that individuals with the gift of grace of prophecy hate evil and have
the ability to identify and define sin. Deborah could not tolerate
living with the Jews and refused to be part of their sin. Deborah and
her husband lived three days away from the Jews in Mount Ephraim
(verse 5).

People with the gift of grace of prophecy hate evil. They also
have a desire to express their message verbally as we can see in verse
6 where it tells us Deborah sent for Barak. Knowing that Barak was
preparing for a large battle, why would Deborah ask him to take a
three day ride one way to her house instead of writing him a letter?
The reason was her concern for the program of God as well as her
desire to give him the message personally.

Verse 4 tells us Deborah was God's judge for the nation of Israel
and was acknowledged as their spiritual leader. The Israelites came
to her for advice. She was also consulted by the local judges from
various tribes who wished to have intractable intertribal disputes
settled.

Deborah received a word of wisdom about Israel's situation. She
summoned Barak and in verses 6 and 7, confronts him with what

God has revealed to her. Barak had already heard and received a battle plan from God. Deborah had spiritually discerned this as we can see in her comment to Barak: "Hath not the Lord God of Israel commanded, saying, Go?..." Barak was afraid so he told Deborah, "If you go I'll go, but if you don't go I won't go." This is not your usual comment from an officer in charge. The person with the gift of grace of prophecy has a concern for the program of God. Barak did not need to twist Deborah's arm to go since she was glad for the opportunity to be assured that things would go as God had planned.

Deborah also probed Barak's conscience and discerned his heart motive. She made it clear that he was not going to receive the glory and honor for the victory in this battle. Deborah reassures Barak in verse 9 that the victory would be the LORD'S, for He was going to do it. Her conversation with Barak was direct and frank as is typical of a person with the gift of grace of prophecy.

As we cover the gift of grace of prophecy, it is noteworthy that both John the Baptist and Deborah were motivated by prophecy as well as being prophets. This does not mean that those with the gift of grace of prophecy will be prophets. Ephesians 4:11 and 1 Corinthians 12:28 make this clear as they inform us that only some have received the ministry gift of a prophet. Using the Bible as our example, we observe that only a few prophets operated during any one period of time in the Jewish nation. Therefore, we can conclude that there are few prophets operating within our Christian community today. Selah!

CHARACTERISTICS OF THE
GIFT OF GRACE OF PROPHECY IN REVIEW

The person with the gift of grace of prophecy has the ability to:

1. See mysteries which are in secret (1 Samuel 9:9; Luke 3:6; Judges 4:6, 7).

2. Probe consciences and manifest secrets that are in the hearts of people, groups and churches (1 Corinthians 14:24, 25; Luke 3:7, 8, 19; Judges 4:9).

3. Hate and define evil (Luke 3:7, 13-16; Judges 4:1). They have an intolerance of doubt, unbelief and spiritual ignorance.

4. Correct by rooting out, pulling down, destroying and throwing down; then they build and plant (Jeremiah 1:5, 9, 10; 1 Corinthians 14:3).

5. Verbally express their message (Luke 3:4; Judges 4:6).

6. Be direct, frank and honest in their conversation (Luke 3; Judges 4; Matthew 11:2, 3).

7. Have a deep concern for the program of God (Judges 4:6, 7; Matthew 11:3).

8. Have a dependence on scriptural truth to validate authority (Matthew 11:2, 3).

The gift of grace of prophecy is a blessing and benefit to the body of Christ. Prophecy is a gift from God that shows us one of His many attributes. When we see this gift operating in the believer, it should remind us that God continues to use the gift of prophecy to bless His children.

The person who has received the gift of grace of prophecy needs to develop it in love, remembering always that after they correct (root out, pull down and destroy) they need to build (repair and make new) and plant (fasten and fortify) of God in love.

5

THE GIFT OF GRACE OF MINISTRY (SERVING)

Or ministry, let us wait on our ministering

Romans 12:7

The word "ministry" used here is *diakonia* in the Greek, signifying a servant (one who attends to the practical needs in connection with service in a local church). People with the gift of grace of ministry are motivated to meet the practical needs of those around them. Hereafter, we will be using the word "serving" as a synonym for ministry.

There is a lot of confusion regarding the gift of grace of serving and the ministry of helps.

Let's look at the definition of these two spiritual gifts:

1. The gift of grace of serving found in Romans 12:7 motivates the believer toward his office in the body of Christ. This

spiritual gift is a motivation or cause to function and operates in the believer from his spiritual birth.

2. The ministry of helps found in 1 Corinthians 12:28 is an office that aids and supports every area of ministry in the local church. For example, ushers, choir members, janitors, musicians, intercessors, secretaries, sound engineers, women's ministries, and other are in the ministry of helps. This office is an avenue to serve any area of need in the church.

The gift of grace of serving motivates believers to act, think, and react to the world around them. The ministry of helps pertains to specific areas of ministry in the church. The ministry of helps and the gift of grace of serving are different gifts, as we can see by their definitions. Although we find the same basic principles, guidelines, and knowledge in scripture apply to both of these spiritual gifts, the basic principles of serving flow through both gifts, though they are exercised differently. The gift of grace of serving is a part of God's personality and motivates the believer toward his ministry office, whereas the ministry of helps is an office that provides particular areas of ministry that aid and support the church. The person with the gift of grace of serving has the ability to aid or support the church by discerning and meeting the practical needs of those around them. Servers have a supernatural ability to discern the needs of those around them. For example, if the church grounds were being neglected, it would not be unusual to find a server who would show up to take care of them. He not only discerns but also fulfills needs. Many believers notice neglected areas in the church but only pray for God to meet the need, whereas a server would take the initiative to personally meet the need. To find out if you are motivated by the gift of grace of serving, take the Gifts of Grace Personal Profile in chapter 12. The questions are directed to find out what gift motivates each believer. The key to finding your gift of grace comes from checking your motivation.

People with the gift of grace of serving are fulfilled when serving someone else. Serving is a part of their personality. There is a joy unspeakable and full of glory when they fulfill the needs of those around them. They are miserable when not involved in a church or serving people. Servers receive joy and fulfillment from the action of serving.

> **Whereof I was made a minister, according to the gift of grace of God given unto me by the effectual working of his power.**
>
> **Ephesians 3:7**

"Minister" used here, in the Greek, is *diakonos* derived from *diako* used in Romans 12:7 and defined as running errands (attendant and waiter). "Effectual" is a derivative of *energema*, meaning efficient energy, which is activated by the believer's gift of grace. Paul states he was created to serve because of his gifts of grace received from God. Gifts of grace are active and operative working as "efficient energies" in the believer by God's supernatural power. People with the gift of grace of serving have God's supernatural power energizing them to accomplish His will (to meet practical needs) in others' lives. Servers have a supernatural energy that allows them to work exceedingly long at reaching God's goals and objectives. For example, servers are most likely to be the first to arrive at a work day or project at the church and the last to leave. In order for this efficient energy to be operative in the server, he must step out and use the gift of grace. People with the gift of grace of serving usually have no problem working for the Kingdom of God since this gift instills a desire and motivation to fulfill the practical needs of those around them.

The pattern or mold for by believers to follow is established by the life and ministry of Jesus Christ, who came not to receive but to give service.

> **For even the Son of Man came not to be ministered (served) unto, but to minister (SERVE), and to give his life a ransom for many.**
>
> **Mark 10:45, explanation mine**

> **But Jesus called them unto him, and said, Ye know that the princes of the Gentiles exercise dominion over them, and they that are great exercise authority upon them. But it shall not be so among you: but whosoever will be great among you, let him be your minister; And whosoever will be chief among you, let him be your servant: Even as the Son of man came not to be ministered unto, but to minister, and to give his life a ransom for many.**
>
> **Matthew 20:25-28**

Jesus tells us in Matthew and Mark that He did not come to be ministered unto. "Minister" is used here in the verb tense of *diakonia* defined as to attend or wait upon. Jesus said He came to serve (minister to) mankind, and as His disciples we should have the same objective. Jesus demonstrates this kind of service in John 13:3-6:

Jesus knowing that the Father had given all things into his hands, and that he was come from God, and went to God; He riseth from supper, and laid aside his garments; and took a towel, and girded himself. After that he poureth water into a basin, and began to wash the disciples' feet, and to wipe them with the towel wherewith he was girded.

Jesus brought the previous scriptures in Matthew and Mark to life when He served His disciples by washing their feet. This is another example of how God meets the practical needs of believers. Jesus Christ followed the example of His master (The Father God) by rendering a loving service to the needs of humanity. God meets all of our needs regardless, if practical or spiritual in nature. People with the gift of grace of serving are concerned for the needs of those around them.

All of the previous scriptures confirm that believers are called to serve. The gift of grace of serving is a gift given by God to profit the body of Christ.

My little children, let us not love in word, neither in tongue; but in deed and truth.

1 John 3:18

John states that love is not only speaking words, but is taking action to needs. The person with the give of grace of serving is a doer of the Word. When a need arises he gets in there and does it.

There are often misunderstandings in the body of Christ relating to God meeting the practical needs of His children. The body of

Christ has leaned heavily on the idea that meeting practical needs is unspiritual. Nowhere can this be substantiated in the Bible. Paul says in Philippians 4:19 that God supplies <u>all of the believers' needs</u> according to His riches in glory by Christ Jesus. The gift of grace of serving is God's avenue to meet the practical needs of the body of Christ.

> **And in those days, when the number of the disciples was multiplied, there arose a murmuring of the Grecians against the Hebrews, because their widows were neglected in the daily ministration. Then the twelve called the multitude of the disciples unto them, and said, It is not reason that we should leave the word of God, and serve tables.**
>
> **Acts 6: 1, 2**

"Ministration" used in verse 1 is the same Greek word found in Romans 12:7 for "ministry" and is defined "to wait upon." These scriptures show us how important it is to meet the practical needs of the body of Christ. Notice, the void in the church was a result of practical needs being neglected. People with the gift of grace of serving have the ability to promote the smooth operation of the church by meeting practical needs, allowing spiritual leaders to fulfill their calling. Typically the gift of grace of serving is portrayed as one of the unspiritual gifts. However, Acts 6:4 states:

> **But we will give ourselves continually to prayer, and to the ministry of the word.**

"Ministry" used here is the same word as in Acts 6:1 for "ministration" which indicates there is no difference between serving tables (meeting practical needs) or ministry of the Word (meeting spiritual needs). There is no difference in importance when service is rendered in the body of Christ. God says He will meet all of your needs. God calls believers to a mutual service within the fellowship of Christ's body. The ability to perform such work is a gift from God the Father.

And I thank Christ Jesus our Lord, who hath enabled (empowered) me, for that he counted me faithful, putting me into the ministry.

1 Timothy 1:12, explanation mine

Jesus Christ put Paul into the ministry and empowered him to fulfill that calling. As we discussed in chapter 2, the recipient of a spiritual gift becomes qualified and responsible using God's ability, strength and power. It is God's responsibility to qualify believers.

As every man hath received the gift, even so minister the same one to another, as good stewards of the manifold grace of God.

1 Peter 4:10

"Minister" used here is the same Greek word as in Romans 12:7. This scripture states every believer has received a gift. The Amplified Bible says this gift is "a particular talent." The purpose of these gifts is to function effectively in a particular service to benefit others in the body of Christ. Every spiritual gift flows through ministry in the church. Let's look at a person who was motivated by the gift of grace of serving:

STEPHEN:

Stephen is an excellent example of a doer of the Word of God, who was motivated by the gift of grace of serving.

And in those days, when the number of disciples was multiplied, there arose a murmuring of the Grecians against the Hebrews, because their widows were neglected in the daily ministration.

Acts 6:1

The church was having problems regarding widows who were neglected. "Ministration" in the Greek is *diakonia*, the same word as "ministry" in Romans 12:7 meaning to wait upon.

Then the twelve called the multitude of the disciples unto them, and said, It is not reason that we should leave the word of God, and serve tables. Wherefore, brethren, look ye out among you seven men of honest report, full of the Holy Ghost and wisdom, whom we may appoint over this business.

Acts 6:2, 3

In verse 2 it tells us the spiritual leaders called for a meeting with the disciples explaining that it was wrong for them to take time away from God's Word to meet the practical needs of the church. It is imperative that the body of Christ realize that God does not expect the pastors and spiritual leaders to fill every need. It isn't that the spiritual leaders did not want to serve the widows but, the problem stemmed from them taking time away from their praying and meditation of the Word. Ephesians 4:16 states, "From whom the whole body fitly joined together and compacted by that which every joint supplieth, according to the effectual working in the measure of every part maketh increase of the body unto the edifying of itself in love." You are a joint and are required to supply according to the measure that God has imparted to you. It is important that you use your measure (limited portion) for it causes you to develop and grow, thereby furthering the Gospel.

The early church under the inspiration of the Holy Spirit elected seven men to oversee this part of church business. These seven men were to serve the body of Christ in meeting practical needs and were called deacons. "Deacon" comes from the Greek word *diakonia*, a minister of service. After the seven men were appointed as deacons, Acts 6:7 states that the Word of God increased and the number of disciples greatly multiplied in Jerusalem. The person with the gift of grace of serving promotes the smooth operation of a church by meeting the practical needs of the body of Christ.

> **And the word of God increased; and the number of the disciples multiplied in Jerusalem greatly; and a great company of the priests were obedient to the faith.**
>
> **Acts 6:7**

When every joint (believer) supplies in the position where God has placed him, there will be an increase in disciples. The Word of God also increases because pastors and spiritual leaders will be able to spend more time in the Word. People who are doers of the Word will move out toward people, resulting in souls being saved and needs being met.

And Stephen, full of faith and power, did great wonders and miracles among the people.

Acts 6:8

Stephen, with the gift of grace of serving, exercised faith and power in meeting the practical needs of the body of Christ. Power in the Greek, is *dunamis* meaning God's miracle working power. Having the gift of grace of serving does not mean you are not spiritual. God requires you to be a servant full of His Spirit and His power.

Some people have taken the gifts of grace and placed them in boxes. I have good news for you; there is more to being a server than potlucks, painting walls, cleaning churches and meeting the practical needs of the church. Stephen, God's example of a server, was a person full of faith and miraculous power who did great wonders and miracles among the people.

But, beloved, we are persuaded better things of you, and things that accompany salvation, though we thus speak. For God is not unrighteous to forget your work and labour of love, which ye have shewed toward his name, in that ye have ministered to the saints, and do minister. And we desire that every one of you do shew the same diligence to the full assurance of hope unto the end.

Hebrews 6:9-11

One important point in this scripture is God will not forget your work and labor of love. There has been a lot of teaching regarding the negative side of the gift of grace of serving. The Bible states in James 1:17 that every gift from the Father God is perfect. A believer having the gift of grace of serving can have problems but the gift itself is perfect. Servers do not have to be constantly patted on the back to continue serving. Actually, people having the gift of grace of serving motivate others to serve. Servers know Colossians 3:24: "Ye serve the Lord Christ." A person with the gift of grace of serving knows he serves Jesus Christ. He does not need to be acknowledged or praised in order to serve. Believers without the gift of grace of serving need to be reminded they serve the Lord and are required to serve in love. Faith works by love and stepping out of love with grumbling and complaining stops the energizing power of God which works through believers. Their faith then becomes stagnant and they are operating in their own fleshly efforts. Paul tells us God does not forget the server's work. Believers must realize their importance, for God rewards servers for their obedience in meeting the needs of the body of Christ. The only time I have found servers grumbling and complaining about their work is when others belittle their gift and accuse them of being unspiritual.

Notice Stephen's beautiful example of walking in LOVE:

> **And cast him out of the city, and stoned him: and the witnesses laid down their clothes at a young man's feet, whose name was Saul. And they stoned Stephen, calling upon God, and saying, Lord Jesus, receive my spirit. And he kneeled down, and cried with a loud voice, Lord, lay not this sin to their charge. And when he had said this, he fell asleep.**
>
> **Acts 7:58-60**

We can see God's forgiveness and love working through Stephen by his words. We are to be motivated by love in everything we do and say.

If you have the gift of grace of serving, pray and ask God what needs He wants you to fill and develop your gift so you will be led by the Spirit and not by the need. Continue to believe that you can be like Stephen, a servant full of faith, energized by love and power doing great wonders and miracles among the people.

If you do not have the gift of grace of serving, pray and ask God to help you become like your Lord who didn't come to be served but to serve mankind. God wants you to be aware of what He has called you to do.

> **Hereby perceive we the love of God, because he laid down his life for us: and we ought to lay down our lives for the brethren. But whoso hath this world's good, and seeth his brother have need, and shutteth up his bowels of compassion from him, how dwelleth the love of God in him? My little children, let us not love in word, neither in tongue; but in deed and in truth.**
>
> **1 John 3: 16-18**

The love of God is shed abroad in the believer's heart and expressed through serving others. A person with the gift of grace of serving demonstrates God's love by serving. John says God's love should be executed in practice and sincerity. Whereas the world's love is by words (theory) only, servers demonstrate God's love by practice and sincerity. God has placed a desire in the server's heart to meet the needs of those around him. The person with the gift of grace of serving has a desire to serve that comes from their innermost being. Inactive servers are unfulfilled and miserable.

Stephen was put in charge of meeting the practical needs of the body of Christ, thereby freeing spiritual leaders to fulfill God's calling on their lives. People with the gift of grace of serving have an ability to be a catalyst for growth by meeting the practical needs of the church, thus freeing spiritual leaders to fulfill their calling. We saw this in Acts 6:4 when servers fulfilled their callings, allowing the spiritual leaders to devote themselves to prayer and ministry of the Word. Stephen's serving led to an increase of the Word of God and in the number of disciples.

Stephen had time to do more than the special work assigned to him, for he was among those foremost in working miracles and preaching the Gospel. The person with the gift of grace of serving has a supernatural ability to accomplish several tasks at once. People motivated by the gift of grace of serving have a supernatural stamina working through them causing them to accomplish God's objectives.

In Acts 6:8, it tells us Stephen worked wonders and miracles among the people. His dedication and service as a servant of God revealed his love for people. A person with the gift of grace of serving has a love for people. Servers are personable; not only do they love people and enjoy serving them but they are also loved by others.

And devout men carried Stephen to his burial and made great lamentation over him.

Acts 8:2

"Lamentation" used here, in the Greek, is defined as to mourn or wail. When Stephen died, his colleagues grieved and mourned for him. People with the gift of grace of serving are easy to love for they spend their lives meeting the needs of others.

WAS MARTHA A SERVER?

No! Martha was <u>not a server</u>. Let's look at why.

> **Now it came to pass, as they went, that he entered into a certain village: and a certain woman named Martha received him into her house. And she had a sister called Mary, which also sat at Jesus' feet, and heard his word. But Martha was cumbered about much serving, and came to him, and said, Lord, dost thou not care that my sister hath left me to serve alone? bid her therefore that she help me. And Jesus answered and said unto her, Martha, Martha, thou art careful and troubled about many things: But one thing is needful: and Mary hath chosen that good part, which shall not be taken away from her.**
>
> **Luke 10:38-42**

Jesus said Mary had chosen the good part, which would not be taken from her. In 1 Corinthians 3, Paul states every man's work will be revealed and no foundation can be laid other than Jesus Christ. Fire will try every man's work; if it stands he shall receive a reward, if not it will be burned and suffer loss. Jesus' comment that Mary's part would not be taken away indicates Mary was fulfilling her calling. The "good part" refers to the foundation laid by Jesus Christ. Martha was not called to be a server; therefore, she was serving in her own fleshly efforts resulting in grumbling and complaining. Jesus did not ask Martha to serve but rather she made the choice. Martha's serving did not produce rewards. Second Corinthians 5:10 states every believer will stand before the judgment seat of Christ and answer for what he has done in his body (good or evil) considering his purpose and motive. If a deed was done without love (through grumbling and complaining) the person will lose his reward.

Martha told Jesus to order Mary to the kitchen because she felt trapped and alone. People with the gift of grace of serving like to complete a project by themselves. Martha's desire to have Mary join her stemmed from sibling jealousy and rivalry. She was miserable when serving and wanted Mary to join in her misery. People with the gift of grace of serving would jump at the chance to serve Jesus in person. Serving Jesus would be the ultimate fulfillment for a server whereas Martha was grumbling and complaining at serving Jesus Christ.

Mary's absence from the kitchen was because she was fulfilling her calling as a teacher in the body of Christ. Mary had spent time at Jesus' feet receiving insight and revelation knowledge about His death and resurrection. Mary had met Jesus as Teacher and High Priest, and she knew He was her Savior.

Choosing to walk in God's predestined plan for your life results in your foundation being on Jesus Christ The work that you do cannot be taken away from you and will result in your receiving a reward. Martha was trying to persuade Jesus to tell Mary to do her bidding. Jesus Christ is the only One who lays the believer's foundation. Mary was called as a teacher, as revealed in John 11:45 where it tells us many Jews believed in Jesus because of Mary. Mary's ability to reveal things of the Lord came from her persistence in being at His feet. Mary had chosen the best part, her place as a teacher in the body of Christ.

CHARACTERISTICS OF THE GIFT OF GRACE OF SERVING IN REVIEW

People with the gift of grace of serving have:

1. A motivation to meet the practical needs of those around them (Romans 12:7).

2. An ability to discern (recognize) and meet the practical needs of those around them (John 13:3-6).

3. The ability to be fulfilled when serving someone else.

4. A supernatural power working through them accomplishing God's will for their life (Ephesians 3:7).

5. A concern for the needs of the people around them (1 John 3:18; John 13:3-6).

6. An ability to be a doer of the Word in meeting practical needs of the body of Christ (1 John 3:18; James 1:22).

7. The ability to be a catalyst for growth by meeting the practical needs of the body of Christ, thus freeing spiritual leaders to fulfill their calling (Acts 6:2, 3; Ephesians 4:16).

8. The ability to promote the smooth operation of the church by meeting the practical needs of the church (Acts 6:7).

9. An assurance that they serve the Lord Christ. They do not need praise to continue serving (Acts 7:58-60; Colossians 3:24).

10. An ability to demonstrate God's love by serving the Word (1 John 3:16-18).

11. A desire to serve that comes from their inner most being (1 John 3:16-18).

12. A supernatural ability to accomplish several tasks at once.

13. The ability to love and care for people (Acts 6:8; Hebrews 6:10).

14. A personality that is easily loved (Acts 8:2).

People with the gift of grace of serving exemplify the life and attitude of our Lord Jesus Christ. As disciples of Christ, they move out toward other people to meet their needs. Servers need to be ruled by peace, accepting themselves as special and unique. The efficient energy that God places in servers allows them to fulfill His call on their life. The gift of grace of serving is desperately needed in the body of Christ for it is not only a tool used by God to meet the practical needs of His church, but also frees spiritual leaders to spend time in prayer and ministry of the Word, thereby fulfilling their calling. The gift of grace of serving was given by God as a blessing and benefit to the body of Christ and to point us back to God who continues to serve and meet all the needs of His children.

6

The Gift Of Grace Of Teaching

...Or he that teacheth, on teaching...

Romans 12:7

The word "teacheth" used here in the Greek, is *didasko* meaning instruction and explanation. The gift of grace of teaching is a motivation to research, instruct, and explain truth. People with the gift of grace of teaching have the ability to seek out, instruct and explain truth. They are motivated by God to study and then enabled by the Holy Spirit of God to instruct and explain learned truths of God. A person with the gift of grace of teaching is fulfilled in revealing the truth.

> **To whom God would make known what is the riches of the glory of this mystery among the Gentiles; which is Christ in you, the hope of glory: Whom we preach, warning every man, and teaching every**

**man in all wisdom; that we may present every man
perfect in Christ Jesus.**

Colossians 1:27, 28

When Paul said "...teaching every man in all wisdom...," he gave us an important principle of teaching. Wisdom is the ability to use or apply knowledge. People with the gift of grace of teaching have the ability to instruct people on application of God's Word to their lives. The purpose being to bring maturity to the body of Christ.

People with the gift of grace of teaching do not deliver prepared information. They are motivated to start from scratch, researching by probing into the Word of God. Then they proceed to instruct and make the Word of God comprehensible. Teachers have a form of doctrine which they use when explaining God's truths.

**But God be thanked, that ye were the servants of
sin, but ye have obeyed from the heart that form of
doctrine.**

Romans 6:17

The Romans had received a form of doctrine. "Doctrine" is *didache* in the Greek meaning instruction or teaching (outline). Even though this Greek word is not the same as "teacheth" in Romans 12:8 it has the same definition. "Form" used here, in the Greek, means pattern or mold. Paul states this form of doctrine was a mold of teaching that caused them to obey the Word of God. People with the gift of grace of teaching mold or shape people in line with God's Word by a form of doctrine. Teachers of the Word of God have the ability to mold the character and conduct of their hearers. They have the ability to fit Christians into scriptural patterns by molding them into a cast or model. In order for something or someone to be molded or shaped, they have to be softened first. For the Christian, this happens through salvation and the baptism of the Holy Spirit as they are softened spiritually. The reason for this spiritual softening is so Christians can be molded and formed into the correct scriptural shapes and patterns. No matter where you are spiritually, you will never outgrow the need for shaping and molding.

There is often confusion between the gift of grace of teaching mentioned in Romans 12:8 and teachers as mentioned in 1 Corinthians 12:28 and Ephesians 4: 11. Having the gift of grace of teaching does NOT mean you are called as a teacher (1 Corinthians 12:28). As we saw earlier, the usage of the word "some" in 1 Corinthians 12:28 informs believers that a certain number are divinely called as teachers in the body of Christ.

Let's look at the definition of these two spiritual gifts:

1. The gift of grace of teaching found in Romans 12:7 motivates believers toward their office in the body of Christ. This spiritual gift is a motivation or cause to function and operates in the believer from their spiritual birth.

2. The teacher mentioned in 1 Corinthians 12:28 and Ephesians 4: 11 is an office of authority that perfects and matures the body of Christ.

We can see by the definitions of the gift of grace of teaching and the office of a teacher that they are two separate, unique gifts although in Scripture we find the same basic principles, guidelines and knowledge flow through both of these gifts.

People with the gift of grace of teaching are very precise and give instruction in a clearly defined form or outline. They become upset upon hearing someone teach without a form of doctrine because of their motivation to teach in order. A true teacher of the Word of God lays a clear outline with no confusion or misunderstanding in their teachings. People with the gift of grace of teaching will take scriptural patterns and fit believers' lives into them, producing the shape and image that God desires.

Let's look at another characteristic found in Romans 6:17. Notice the last half of the verse says, "but ye have obeyed from the heart the form of doctrine which was delivered you." "Delivered" is *paradidomi* in the Greek meaning to transmit. People with the gift of grace of teaching have the ability to transmit their knowledge to the believer in an understandable and usable way. Teachers have the ability to research the Word of God and gain wisdom and revelation knowledge. They then transmit their knowledge and understanding to the recipient. God's teachers have the ability to hand over their knowledge. This is a supernatural ability given by God to mature the body of Christ. If a person in a teaching position does not have this ability, then he must realize he is functioning in his own fleshly efforts and not by a calling of God. Teachers make the Word of God comprehensible thereby encouraging and exhorting believers to live by God's Word.

This brings us to the last characteristic found in Romans 6:17 where it says, "ye have obeyed from the heart." Paul tells us teachers have the ability to make believers obey the Word of God from their hearts. Teachers can deliver the Word of God in away that causes believers to obey it from their heart. Christians desire to mold and pattern themselves after the form of doctrine that has been presented to them by teachers of the Word of God. Teachers lay down God's mold in an attractive and pleasant manner that persuades Christians to obey from their heart, causing them to make decisions that will produce fruits of righteousness in their lives.

> **But now being made free from sin, and become servants to God, ye have your fruit unto holiness, and the end everlasting life.**
>
> **Romans 6:22**

God's form of doctrine is never negative but always edifies and builds up His children. As we saw in the chapter on prophecy, even after God gives correction, He exhorts, encourages, and comforts. Teaching God's truths will always produce fruits of righteousness and holiness.

Let's look at biblical examples of two individuals with the gift of grace of teaching.

APOLLOS:

> **And a certain Jew named Apollos, born at Alexandria, an eloquent man, and mighty in the scriptures, came to Ephesus. This man was instructed in the way of the Lord; and being fervent in the spirit, he**

131

spake and taught diligently the things of the Lord, knowing only the baptism of John. And he began to speak boldly in the synagogue: whom when Aquila and Priscilla had heard, they took him unto them, and expounded unto him the way of God more perfectly. And when he was disposed to pass into Achaia, the brethren wrote, exhorting the disciples to receive him: who, when he was come, helped them much which had believed through grace: For he mightily convinced the Jews, and that publicly, shewing by the scriptures that Jesus was Christ.

Acts 18:24-28

The first characteristic of the gift of grace of teaching in Apollos' life is found in verse 24 where it tells us he was an "eloquent man." "Eloquent" means learned, in the Greek. People with the gift of grace of teaching are educated in the Word of God and have the ability to speak effectively. Apollos' ability as an outstanding and effective speaker was because of the gift of grace of teaching. Notice verse 24 also tells us he was "mighty in the scriptures," revealing to us his knowledge of the Word of God. "Mighty" means powerful in the Greek. People with the gift of grace of teaching have the ability to be persuasive due to their knowledge of the Word of God and wisdom. We can see Apollos' ability in verse 28 where he mightily convinced the Jews publicly, showing them Jesus was Christ. Apollos was well grounded in the Scriptures which enabled the Holy Spirit to work through him mightily in persuading the Jews that Jesus was Christ, the Messiah. People having the gift of grace of teaching have a sound understanding of the Bible. Scripture is the whole foundation of the teaching ministry. Teachers are required by God to have extensive biblical knowledge. This is logical since they cannot teach unless they have the knowledge to reveal the truth to the body of Christ.

Paul warns the body of Christ to be careful not to get puffed up with knowledge.

> **...knowledge puffeth up, but charity edifieth.**
> **1 Corinthians 8: 1**

Teachers especially need to be careful of this stumbling block. "Puffed up" means to swell up with pride (self-sufficient) in the Greek context. The ability to study and then transmit knowledge comes from God as a blessing and service to the body of Christ. Teachers need to realize their ability is supernatural and given for the purpose of serving the body of Christ.

> **Not that we are sufficient of ourselves to think any-
> thing as of ourselves; but our sufficiency is of God;
> who also hath made us able ministers of the New
> Testament; not of the letter, but of the spirit: for the
> letter killeth, but the spirit giveth life.**
> **2 Corinthians 3:5-6**

Our sufficiency is of God because He has made us able ministers of the New Testament. Our ability is from God working through us by His Spirit. God says it's not by might nor by power but by His Spirit. God's Spirit working through the believer is activated by His gift of grace. Paul always gave God credit for what He accomplished in his life. He realized it was God who was at work in him both to will and do His good pleasure.

In Acts 18:25, it says Apollos was instructed in the way of the Lord showing us he was teachable. People with the gift of grace of teaching have a teachable spirit. We can see Apollos was teachable because the Bible tells us he received Priscilla and Aquila taking him aside and expounding the way of God more perfectly (verse 26). Teachers make excellent students because of their desire to know more of God.

The scriptures written on Apollos reveal his personality to us, telling us he was fervent in the spirit and taught diligently. "Fervent," in the Greek context means "hot and boiling." Apollos had a strong personality and was bold in spirit. Teachers speak with authority and boldness. Apollos taught diligently meaning accurately and systematically. Teachers will take you line upon line and precept upon precept since they are motivated to be accurate and systematic. Teachers have a hard time opening a discussion after their teaching because people ask questions that do not pertain to the outline that has just been given. Teachers follow their outlines exactly because of their strict regimentation.

Paul said he planted and Apollos watered. Paul was an apostle (one of his many offices in the body of Christ) sent forth by God into virgin territory to preach and teach about Jesus Christ. Paul's gift of grace of prophecy motivated him toward his office. People with the gift of grace of teaching have the desire and ability to spiritually feed the flock of God. They love to see people born again but their hearts' desire is to deal with Christians by expounding on God's truths. Apollos' desire to water sprang from his gift of grace of teaching that was motivating him toward feeding God's flock.

This study on spiritual gifts gives us a better understanding of people in the body of Christ. We can appreciate that God created every believer as an individual who will produce unique effects. Every person has been created as an original with a divine plan for his life. Though we are individuals, we have been created to work as a team which can be seen by Paul's comment in 1 Corinthians 3:6 that he and Apollos both had a job to do but God was in charge. Christians must realize God places them in the body as it pleases Him.

The last characteristic we find in Apollos' life is found in Acts 18:27:

> **who, when he was come, helped them much which had believed...**

Apollos helped those who believed. People with the gift of grace of teaching have a unique insight into the needs in the body of Christ. They have the capability to help the body of Christ by giving them practical revelation knowledge that can be used in their everyday lives.

MARY:

> **Now it came to pass, as they went, that he entered into a certain village: and a certain woman named Martha received him into her house. And she had a sister called Mary, which also sat at Jesus' feet and heard His Word. But Martha was cumbered about**

much serving, and came to him, and said, Lord, dost thou not care that my sister hath left me to serve alone? bid her therefore that she help me. And Jesus answered and said unto her, Martha, Martha, thou art careful and troubled about many things: But one thing is needful: and Mary hath chosen that good part, which shall not be taken away from her.

Luke 10:38-42

Notice that Mary sat at Jesus' feet listening to His Word. A teacher of the Word of God is required to spend time with the Lord in His Word. It takes a lot of time to research and probe into God's Word in order to be qualified to expound on biblical truths. Mary had spent time at Jesus' feet receiving insight and revelation knowledge. In verse 42, Jesus tells Martha that Mary had chosen the good part that would not be taken away from her. The good part Jesus refers to is her place in the body of Christ. Mary had the gift of grace of teaching, that's why she needed to be at Jesus' feet. Mary's place in the body of Christ was not the same as Martha's.

It is imperative that the body of Christ see themselves as individual members created to be originals entrusted with talent, abilities, and spiritual gifts that produce unique effects in furthering the Gospel.

Then when Mary was come where Jesus was, and saw him, she fell down at his feet, saying unto him, Lord, if thou hadst been here, my brother had not died. When Jesus therefore saw her weeping, and the Jews also weeping which came with her, he groaned

in the spirit, and was troubled, And said, where have ye laid him? They said unto him, Lord come and see. Jesus wept. Then said the Jews, Behold how he loved him!

John 11:32-36

In verse 32 we can see Mary expressing doubt and unbelief, and in verse 33, we can see the Jews and Mary crying. This caused Jesus to groan in the spirit and to become troubled. Jesus' grief stemmed from Mary's and the Jews' response of doubt and unbelief. They had spent many hours sitting under His teachings and still didn't understand. Jesus expected Mary to understand His death and resurrection because of the time she had spent learning about Him. Her response of doubt and unbelief caused Jesus to cry in verse 35. After Lazarus was raised from the dead, Mary finally understood Jesus' death and resurrection, for John 11:45 tells us:

Then many of the Jews which came to Mary, and had seen the things which Jesus did, believed on him.

The Jews came to Mary because they knew she had spent time with the greatest teacher the world will ever know, Jesus Christ. Mary met Jesus as her Teacher and High Priest, and knew that He was her Lord and Savior. Mary's insight stemmed from the time she had spent at her Lord's feet listening to His Word. Mary had the ability to reveal God's truths because she had chosen the best part (her place as a teacher in the body of Christ). It is essential that you find out where God has placed you in His body so you can give maximum purpose to your life by being in a place where you will be the most effective.

CHARACTERISTICS OF THE GIFT OF GRACE OF TEACHING IN REVIEW

The person with the gift of grace of teaching:

1   Has the ability to seek out, instruct, and explain truth (Romans 12:8).

2. Has the ability to mold and shape people in line with God's Word by a form of doctrine (Romans 6: 17).

3. Has the ability to take scriptural patterns and fit Christian's lives into them, thus producing the shape and image God desires (Romans 6:17).

4. Has the ability to transmit knowledge to believers in an understandable and usable way (Romans 6:17).

5. Has the ability to bring Christians to a point of obedience resulting in fruits of righteousness and holiness (Acts 18:28, John 11:45).

6. Is educated in the Word of God and can speak effectively (Acts 18:24).

7. Has a teachable spirit because of their desire to expound on God's truths (Acts 18:26, Luke 10:39).

8. Has the desire and ability to spiritually feed the flock of God (1 Corinthians 3:6, Acts 18:27).

THE GIFT OF GRACE
OF EXHORTATION

Or he that exhorteth, on exhortation...

Romans 12:8

"Exhortation," in the Greek, is *paraklesis* meaning one who encourages, beseeches, consoles, and comforts. *Paraklesis* derives its nature from the Greek word *parakletos*, a term that applies to the Holy Spirit. We have carried *parakletos* over into the English language and refer to the Holy Spirit as the *Paraclete*. When we speak of the Holy Spirit as our paraclete it refers to one who is called alongside to help. He (the Holy Spirit) helps believers by encouraging, comforting, consoling, and exhorting. The Holy Spirit has a ministry of exhortation. He is called along-side to help us by stimulating our faith and exhorting us to act upon it. Another name for the Holy Spirit is the Comforter. People with the gift of grace of exhortation help the body of Christ by comfort, consolation and encouragement. They have a strong desire to communicate their faith to other Christians and see them come into a stable and consistent life.

Let's see how the Word of God defines exhortation. We're going to look at the epistle of Paul to Philemon which gives characteristics of the exhorter.

Hearing of thy love and faith, which thou hast toward the Lord Jesus, and toward all saints; That the communication of thy faith may become effectual by the acknowledging of every good thing which is in you in Christ Jesus. For we have great joy and consolation in thy love, because the bowels of the saints are refreshed by thee, brother.

Philemon 5-7

In verse 7, the word "consolation" is the same word in the Greek as exhortation in Romans 12:8. Let's see Paul's definition of an exhorter. Notice in verse 5 Paul tells us of the love and faith that Philemon has toward the Lord Jesus and all the saints. People with the gift of grace of exhortation love and have faith in the Lord Jesus and people. Philemon was known for his love and faith not only toward the Lord Jesus Christ but also toward his fellow saints. A person with the gift of grace of exhortation focuses on people and their spiritual growth and progress. The desire of the exhorter is to minister and bless people.

In verse 6, Paul says exhorters have the ability to communicate their faith and urge people to a full maturity in Christ. People with the gift of grace of exhortation have the ability to transmit their faith, causing growth in the recipient's life. Paul lists two more characteristics of an exhorter in verse 7 where he states they have "great joy" and "consolation in refreshing the bowels of the saints." Notice Paul says Philemon gave them great joy and consolation in his love for them. People with the gift of grace of exhortation have the ability to bring great joy and consolation to believers. The Word tells us love never fails and a perfect example of this is Philemon. The last characteristic of an exhorter as found in Philemon is "the bowels of the saints are refreshed." The definition of "refreshed" in the Greek, is to take an intermission from labor or to give rest. People with the gift of grace of exhortation have the ability to strengthen and refresh the bowels (the innermost part) of believers.

It is noteworthy that in verse 6, Paul uses the word "effectual" which is energes in the Greek, derived from the word *energema* meaning active, operative, and powerful. In chapter 2, we studied energema and found that the gifts of grace work in believers by God's energizing power. Paul states that Philemon's ability to encourage, console and comfort the saints comes from the gift of grace of exhortation that is working in him. The gift of grace of exhortation working in the believer motivates him toward people.

The main emphasis of the gift of grace of teaching is on researching and revealing truth. Revealing the truth for the exhorter is the beginning of his fulfillment. The exhorter then goes beyond revealing the truth with an intense interest in the individual and how he is receiving the truth. His interest is that believers walk in the truth. When a believer motivated by teaching finishes his form or guideline, he is satisfied to stop there. However, a believer motivated by exhortation will continue to minister until he feels every person has been built up and edified on an individual basis.

Let's look at another biblical example of an exhorter.

PETER:

And with many other words did he testify and exhort, saying, Save yourselves from this untoward generation.

Acts 2:40

This is the end of Peter's sermon on the day of Pentecost. Notice it says with many other words did Peter testify and exhort. People with the gift of grace of exhortation use many words to express an idea. The reason for the exhorter's verbosity is their desire to see the Word become flesh in the believer's life. Their motivation to stimulate faith comes from the gift of grace of exhortation. Let's see how Peter's life correlates with the characteristics of the gift of grace of exhortation.

So when they had dined, Jesus saith to Simon Peter, Simon, son of Jonas, lovest thou me more than these? He saith unto him, yea, Lord; thou knowest that I love thee. He saith unto him, Feed my lambs. He saith unto him again the second time, Simon, son of Jonas, lovest thou me? He saith unto him, Yea, Lord: thou knowest that I love thee. He saith unto him, Feed my sheep. He saith unto him the third time, Lovest thou me?... And he said unto

him, Lord, thou knowest all things; thou knowest that I love thee. Jesus said unto him, feed my sheep.

John 21:15-17

Peter was grieved because Jesus asked him three times if he loved him. Peter's comment, "Lord, You know all things," reveals his defense. One of the characteristics of an exhorter is that he loves the Lord Jesus Christ. We can see in these verses the intimate love Peter had for Jesus.

We also have another characteristic of exhortation shown by the example of Peter's faith in the Lord Jesus found in Matthew 16:15-17:

He saith unto them, But whom say ye that I am? And Simon Peter answered and said, Thou art the Christ, the Son of the living God. And Jesus answered and said unto him, Blessed art thou, Simon Barjona: for flesh and blood hath not revealed it unto thee, but my Father which is in heaven.

Peter's statement is regarding his faith in Jesus being Christ the Messiah, the Son of the living God.

Peter wrote two epistles out of his love for the saints exhorting them on how to live. Chapter 1 of Peter's first epistle exhorts them on how to face trials. Chapter 2 instructs them on how to live a life of holiness (how to please God). In chapter 3, he uses Jesus Christ and His relationship with the Church to exhort husbands and wives on how they should treat one another. In chapter 4, Peter exhorts believers to walk in divine love when working with one another in the church. Peter concludes in chapter 5 with an exhortation to elders to rule in love, then he gives salutations and a benediction. Peter's epistles reveal characteristic of an exhorter.

Let's look at areas the person with the gift of grace of exhortation might address to exhort others to live a life pleasing to God.

1. HOW TO PLEASE GOD:

> **Furthermore then we beseech you, brethren, and exhort you by the Lord Jesus, that as ye have received of us how ye ought to walk and how to please God, so ye would abound more and more.**
>
> **1 Thessalonians 4:1**

"Exhort" used here, in the Greek, is the same word as "exhorteth" in Romans 12:8. The word "beseech" is a synonym of "exhortation."

Other reference scriptures you can consult are Hebrews 11:6 and 2 Timothy 2:21.

2. HOW ONE OUGHT TO LIVE:

> **I beseech you therefore brethren, by the mercies of God, that ye present your bodies a living sacrifice, holy, acceptable until God, which is your reasonable service.**
> **And be not conformed to this world: but be transformed by the renewing of your mind, that ye may prove what is that good, and acceptable, and perfect, will of God.**
>
> **Romans 12:1,2**

3. HOW TO PROGRESS IN LOVE:

But as touching brotherly love ye need not that I write unto you: for ye yourselves are taught of God to love one another. And indeed ye do it toward all the brethren which are in all Macedonia: but we beseech you, brethren, that ye increase more and more.

1 Thessalonians 4:9,10

"Beseech" used here, in the Greek, is the same word for "exhorteth" found in Romans 12:8.

Other reference scriptures you can consult are Galatians 5:13, 14; Ephesians 3:17-19; Ephesians 4:15; Philippians 1:9-11.

4. HOW TO LIVE A LIFE WORTHY OF GOD:

As ye know how we exhorted and comforted and charged every one of you, as a father doth his children, that ye would walk worthy of God , who hath called you into his kingdom and glory.

1 Thessalonians 2:11, 12

Another reference scripture is Ephesians 4:1,2.

5. HOW TO FACE TRIALS:

Confirming the souls of the disciples, and exhorting them to continue in the faith, and that we must through much tribulation enter into the kingdom of God.

Acts 14:22

Other reference scriptures you can consult are 2 Corinthians 4:8-14 and Romans 5:3-5.

6. HOW TO UNDERSTAND CHASTENING:

For consider him that endured such contradiction of sinners against himself, lest ye be wearied and faint in your minds. Ye have not yet resisted unto blood, striving against sin. And ye have forgotten the exhortation which speaketh unto you as unto children, My son, despise not thou the chastening of the Lord, nor faint when thou art rebuked of Him.

Hebrews 12:3-5

The word "chastening" defined in the Greek is education by training or disciplinary correction.

Another reference scripture you can consult is Ephesians 5:26.

Understanding the gifts of grace is imperative for believers in order to promote spiritual growth in the body of Christ. One person failing to function in his place causes a void, leaving the body of Christ less effective. For example, without teaching how would exhortation expound on the truth and stimulate the believer to walk in it? The body of Christ needs all of the gifts of grace in operation. God gave the gifts of grace to the body of Christ to meet all the members' needs.

Let's look at some more characteristics of the gift of exhortation exemplified through Peter's life. Peter's second epistle was written to warn Christians against false teachers.

Wherefore I will not be negligent to put you always in remembrance of these things, though ye know them, and be established in the present truth. Yea, I think it meet, as long as I am in this tabernacle, to stir you up by putting you in remembrance.

2 Peter 1 : 12, 13

Peter states that as long as he remains alive, he will bring them in remembrance of the Word of God in order to establish them. How did Peter motivate the Christians to become grounded and rooted in the Word of God? It tells us in verse 13 he stirred them up. People with the gift of grace of exhortation have the ability to awaken believers to walk in the truth. "Stir" in the Greek means to fully awaken or arouse. Having the ability to stir people up shows Peter had an outgoing personality. He used this God-given ability to stimulate believers to walk in God's truths. Peter wasn't satisfied to stop after revealing God's truths, but went on to stimulate their faith to walk in these truths. Peter continued to exhort believers to pursue excellence in every area of their lives, producing stability and spiritual growth. Peter accurately and enthusiastically illuminated God's Word in his epistles, which continue even today to comfort, console, and encourage Christians.

This second epistle, beloved, I now write unto you; in both which I stir up your pure minds by way of remembrance.

2 Peter 3:1

This is another demonstration of Peter's love and faith toward the saints. He calls them beloved. Notice how he uses the word "pure" to describe their minds, indicating his faith and trust in Christians. "Pure" is *eilikrines* in the Greek, meaning judged and found as genuine and sincere. Peter had found his fellow Christians to be genuine and out of his love for them he wrote his second epistle to exhort and stir (stimulate) their faith by communicating his faith in biblical principles. People with the gift of grace of exhortation are concerned and mindful people.

BARNABAS:

> **And Joses, who by the apostles was surnamed Barnabas, (which is, being interpreted, the son of consolation,) a Levite, and of the country of Cyprus, having land, sold it, and brought the money, and laid it at the apostles' feet.**
>
> **Acts 4:36, 37**

Barnabas was known as the Son of Consolation. "Consolation" as we studied in the beginning of this chapter is one of the definitions of "exhortation." Barnabas gave the money received from the sale of his property to the apostles as an example before the saints to stimulate their faith motivating them to do likewise.

> **And when Saul was come to Jerusalem, he assayed to join himself to the disciples: but they were all afraid of him, and believed not that he was a disciple. But Barnabas took him, and brought him to the apostles, and declared unto them how he had seen the Lord in the way, and that he had spoken to**

him, and how he had preached boldly at Damascus in the name of Jesus.

Acts 9:26, 27

Verse 26 shows the disciples' lack of trust concerning Saul. Barnabas, on the other hand, defended Saul to the disciples because of his gift of grace of exhortation. People with the gift of grace of exhortation love people and are willing to believe the best of a person. This is confirmed in Acts 15:37-39 where Barnabas defends John Mark to Paul. Barnabus being an exhorter, had faith in John Mark as a disciple of Jesus Christ. John Mark had departed early from a missionary journey, an action which Paul considered irresponsible. Paul, motivated by the gift of grace of prophecy, wanted to correct and discipline John Mark whereas Barnabas being an exhorter, wanted to allow John Mark to start over.

Who when he came, and had seen the grace of God, was glad, and exhorted them all, that with purpose of heart they would cleave unto the Lord. For he was a good man, and full of the Holy Ghost and of faith: and much people was added unto the Lord.

Acts 11:23, 24

Barnabus exhorted them to yield their will to God's will and live a life pleasing to God. People with the gift of grace of exhortation have the ability to encourage individuals to pursue a certain course of conduct by helping them visualize God's best.

Confirming the souls of the disciples, and exhorting them to continue in the faith, and that we must

through much tribulation enter into the kingdom of God.

Acts 14:22

Barnabas exhorted the disciples by encouraging them to continue in the faith and not let trials discourage their walk with God.

CHARACTERISTICS OF THE GIFT
OF GRACE OF EXHORTATION IN REVIEW

The person with the gift of grace of exhortation:

1. Helps the body of Christ with comfort, consolation, and encouragement (Romans 12:8).

2. Has love and faith in the Lord Jesus Christ and all the saints (Philemon 5; John 21:15-17; Matthew 16:15-17).

3. Has the ability to transmit his faith, causing spiritual growth in the recipient's life (Philemon 6; Matthew 16:15-17; 1 Peter 1:12, 13; Acts 2: 14-42).

4. Has the ability to bring great joy and consolation to believers (Philemon 7; Acts 4:36).

5. Has the ability to strengthen and refresh the bowels (the innermost part) of believers (Philemon 7; Acts 18:23).

6. Uses many words to express an idea (Acts 2:40).

7. Exhorts people to live a life pleasing to God.

8. Has the ability to awaken believers to walk in the truth (2 Peter 1:12, 13; 2 Peter 3:1).

9. Is concerned for and mindful of people (2 Peter 3:1).

10. Loves people and is willing to believe the best of a person (Acts 9:26, 27).

11. Has the ability to encourage individuals to a certain course of conduct by helping them visualize God's best (Acts 11:23, 24).

The gift of grace of exhortation is an expression of the Holy Spirit who enables us to see the God of Comfort continuing to exhort, console and comfort His children.

8

THE GIFT OF GRACE OF GIVING

...He that giveth, let him do it with simplicity....

Romans 12:8

The word "giveth" used here, in the Greek, is *metadidomi*. *Meta* meaning "with others" and *didomi* meaning "to give, share, or impart." Giving, therefore in the Greek, is the spending out of one's life with others. Notice the purpose of giving is to share with others. As we saw in chapter 2, God's spiritual gifts are to benefit others. People with the gift of grace of giving are given the motivation by God to support the body of Christ.

Many Christians have misunderstood the definition of giving, believing it only refers to money and material possessions. Many people immediately upon hearing the word "give" think only of money; this is incorrect since giving involves much more than money and material possessions. For example, when you hear the statement "God is a giver," do you limit your thoughts to money and material possessions? Of course not, because God enables you to see a broader scope. God meets all of your needs (spiritual, physical, emotional, and financial) according to His riches in glory by Christ Jesus. God never limits His giving to material assets, but instead uses giving as an avenue (one of many) in which He blesses His children. In Psalm 103:2 David says: "Bless the Lord, O my soul, and forget not all his benefits." Let's look at some scriptures that expound on God's benefits through this gift.

> **For I long to see you, that I may impart unto you some spiritual gift, to the end ye may be established.**
>
> **Romans 1:11**

"Impart" used here, in the Greek, is *metadidomi*, the same word used for giveth in Romans 12:8. This scripture has nothing to do with money for Paul says, "I want to see you so I can give you something spiritual." His purpose for imparting a spiritual gift was to establish the Romans. People with the gift of grace of giving have a desire to impart spiritual gifts so the body of Christ is established.

> **So being affectionately desirous of you, we were willing to have imparted unto you, not the gospel of God only, but also our own souls, because ye were dear unto us.**
>
> **1 Thessalonians 2:8**

"Imparted" used here, in the Greek, is also *metadidomi*. "Souls" is defined in the Greek as to breathe life. Paul says they were willing to give not only the Gospel but also the breath of life from their own souls unto the Thessalonians because of their love for them. Love motivated their willingness to share beyond just their knowledge of God in meeting the needs of believers.

And this they did, not as we hoped, but first gave their own selves to the Lord and unto us by the will of God.

2 Corinthians 8:5

People motivated to give are willing to share their life, time and money with the body of Christ. Notice Paul said they first gave of themselves to the Lord and then to the body of Christ. All of the gifts of grace work through believers as they yield and respond to Christ's ability in them to perform. Paul realized that without Jesus Christ working through him, he would not be able to share himself with others.

Many people have no problem when it comes to giving their money to God, but are not willing to give of themselves or their time. People with the gift of grace of giving are willing to share of themselves, their time and money for the work of the Lord.

He that hath two coats, let him impart to him that hath none: and he that hath meat, let him do likewise.

Luke 3:11

"Impart" is the same Greek word as "giveth" in Romans 12:8. People having the gift of grace of giving have a desire and are willing to share materially with someone else in order to supply and support them. Notice this scripture does not imply you have to have an over-abundance of material things in order to give. The world thinks of prosperity as being wealthy, yet Paul defines it differently.

> **And God is able to make all grace abound toward you; that ye, always having all sufficiency in all things, may abound to every good work.**
>
> **2 Corinthians 9:8**

Prosperity is having enough for all your needs and more, so you can give to every good work. God's will for believers is that all of their needs be met by His riches in glory by Christ Jesus. Yet God doesn't stop there, He gives you more than enough so you can share with others.

> **Let him that stole steal no more: but rather let him labour, working with his hands the thing which is good, that he may have to give to him that needed.**
>
> **Ephesians 4:28**

"Give" used here, in the Greek, is also *metadidomi*, the same word used in Romans 12:8 for "giveth." People with the gift of grace of giving are willing to work with their hands so that they can give to those in need. Paul uses the giver as an excellent example of one who uses his abilities (working with his hands) to do good instead of evil (one who steals). We're going to cover this later when we study Dorcas, God's example of a giver.

People with the gift of grace of giving have no problem with tithing, offerings, and almsdeeds. "Tithes" found in Malachi 3:10, is *maarah* in the Hebrew meaning a tenth. God requires Christians to tithe a tenth of their income. "Offerings," found in Malachi 3:8 is *terumah* in the Hebrew meaning gifts of sacrifice signifying giving above the tithe. The practical aspect of offerings is that they provide added financial support for the church. "Almsdeed," found in Acts 9:36, is *eleemosume* in the Greek meaning merciful giving directed toward the poor. The person with the gift of grace of giving loves to give and does it cheerfully as unto the Lord. Givers are always ready to share.

Let's look at key scriptures that define other characteristics of the giver.

> **How that in a great trial of affliction the abundance of their joy and their deep poverty abounded unto the riches of their liberality. For to their power, I bear record, yea, and beyond their power they were willing of themselves; Praying us with much entreaty that we would receive the gift, and take upon us the fellowship of the ministering to the saints.**
>
> **2 Corinthians 8:2-4**

We can see that the churches of Macedonia were going through a severe financial trial. Paul was delighted that they were not caught up in their needs and uses them as an example to motivate other believers to give. The churches of Macedonia knew their trials were temporal and subject to change and this motivated them to keep their eyes fixed and focused on God's promises.

**He that observeth the wind shall not sow; and he
that regardeth the clouds shall not reap.**

Ecclesiastes 11:4

A person who looks for circumstances to be perfect in order to give will never give. People who are motivated by the gift of grace of giving have the ability to look past their circumstances and continue to give. Trials do not affect their giving because they have supernatural ability (power) working through them, motivating them to give.

In 2 Corinthians 8:2, we see that with an abundance of joy they liberally gave, even in their poverty. Many Christians not motivated by the gift of grace of giving will stop tithing at the first sign of financial problems. We see that the Macedonian churches went beyond their power. "Power" used here, in the Greek, is defined as ability. The Macedonians yielded to God's ability in them to accomplish His will.

Let's look at 2 Corinthian 8:4 in the Amplified Bible:

**Begging us most insistently for the favor and the
fellowship of contributing in this ministration for
the relief and support of the saints in Jerusalem.**

The believers not only begged but insisted that Paul and his fellow laborers receive their contribution to aid and support their fellow saints in Jerusalem. "Ministration," as seen here is the same Greek word for ministry found in Romans 12:7 and defined as servant. Their contribution enabled Paul and his fellow laborers to continue to serve the saints in Jerusalem. Let's look at 2 Corinthians 8: 11, 12.

Now therefore perform the doing of it; that as there was a readiness to will, so there may be a performance also out of that which ye have. For if there be first a willing mind, it is accepted according to that a man hath, and not according to that he hath not.

Notice Paul says "there was a readiness to will," referring to giving indicating they were already motivated to give. People with the gift of grace of giving have a readiness to give. "Readiness" in the Greek is *prothumia* meaning an eager willingness or forwardness. They were not shy about their giving because the definition shows their ability to be forward. Paul encourages Christians in Corinth to have that same eager and willing mind to give. The Macedonians did not give begrudgingly or out of necessity. Paul says believers are to give according to what they have and not according to what they don't have. In 2 Corinthians 9:7 Paul goes on to say, "Every man according as he purposeth in his heart, so let Him give not grudgingly, or of necessity; for God loves a cheerful giver." A person giving of necessity has the wrong heart motive of desperation and not willingness. God says He loves a cheerful giver. "Cheerful," in the Greek, is *hilaros* meaning prompt, happy, willing. The word hilarious is derived from the Greek work *hilaros*. God wants to see His children give with a readiness of mind and a hilarious heart. People with the gift of grace of giving are fulfilled when aiding and supporting people in the body of Christ. They are eager and willing because of their motivation to give of themselves, their time and money to the work of the Lord.

It is not how much people give to the church that determines if they are givers. Givers are people who yield themselves, their time and everything they have as a living sacrifice unto God. The Bible tells us in Romans 12:1 that this is our reasonable service unto God. Many Christians think they are not givers because they are not wealthy. Financial prosperity is not the key ingredient for a giver. Second Corinthians 8:12 says there first must be a willing mind, then it is accepted according to what a man has and not what he has not. The Bible tells us the key ingredient to look for in a giver is the willingness of mind. If there is a willingness of mind then the gift is accepted, not on the basis of what a person doesn't have but on the basis of what he does have. The person with this gift of grace is willing to share whatever he has to support the Kingdom of God.

Let's look at scriptures that expound on giving:

And Jesus sat over against the treasury, and beheld the people cast money into the treasury: and many that were rich cast in much. And there came a certain poor widow, and she threw in two mites, which make a farthing. And he called unto him his disciples, and saith unto them, Verily, I say unto you, that this poor widow hath cast more in, than all they which have cast into the treasury; for all they did cast in of their abundance; but she of her want did cast in all that she had, even all her living.

Mark 12:41-44

"Beheld" in the Greek means to be a spectator of, discern, consider, and look upon. Jesus watched the people as they gave into the treasury. Jesus Christ is the same yesterday, today and forever. He's still watching the heart motives of people as they give into the Kingdom of God. The key words in these scriptures are "cast" and "threw," the difference being threw is more violent. The widow threw her two mites in, indicating her eager and willing mind. Jesus said she gave out of what she had and not out of her abundance. Those two mites thrown into the treasury were her living, showing us her heart motive was to share what she had with others. Many who were rich gave large sums of money out of their abundance but the quantity is not what impressed Jesus since He looks at the heart motive. The widow could have looked at her money and realized it was her living causing her to fear. Jesus was impressed because she chose to throw her money in, signifying she wasn't caught up in the cares of this world but trusted the Giver to supply her needs.

> **But this I say, He which soweth sparingly shall reap also sparingly; and he which soweth bountifully shall reap also bountifully. Every man according as he purposeth in his heart, so let him give; not grudgingly, or of necessity: for God loveth a cheerful giver. And God is able to make all grace abound toward you; that ye, always having all sufficiency in all things, may abound to every good work.**
>
> **2 Corinthians 9:6-8**

Paul tells us a stingy giver will receive a meager reward, but he who gives generously receives an open-handed reward. The Lord judges givers by their heart motive. People giving to the Lord should do it out of an eager and willing heart, not out of a need or envy because the Father God loves a cheerful giver. After you decide in your heart to be a cheerful, prompt-to-do giver, God is able to meet all your needs in sufficiency so you will have enough to give to every good work. People with the gift of grace of giving are motivated cheerfully to give out of a purposeful and determined heart.

Let's look at another characteristic of the gift of grace of giving.

> **Being enriched in everything to all bountifulness, which causeth through us thanksgiving to God. For the administration of this service not only supplieth the want of the saints, but is abundant also by many thanksgivings unto God.**
>
> **2 Corinthians 9:11, 12**

People with the gift of grace of giving render a service to the body of Christ that supplies the needs and wants of the saints. They are motivated to discern and meet the needs of those who are lacking in the body of Christ. This service causes the body of Christ to give thanks to the Father God for meeting their needs. Remember, the gifts of grace are an extension of our Lord, given to the body of Christ to supply all of their needs.

> **For I know the forwardness of your mind, for which I boast of you to them of Macedonia, that Achaia was ready a year ago; and your zeal hath provoked very many.**
>
> **2 Corinthians 9:2**

"Provoked" used here, in the Greek, is *erethizo* meaning to stimulate. Paul said their zealous to give enthusiastically (forwardness of mind) stimulated others to give. People with the gift of grace of giving are a catalyst for prompting others in the body of Christ to be cheerful givers.

The gift of grace of giving motivates a person to follow Christ by moving out toward people in meeting their needs. Let's look at God's example of a giver in the life of Dorcas.

DORCAS:

> Now there was in Joppa a certain disciple named Tabitha, which by interpretation is called Dorcas: this woman was full of good works and almsdeeds which she did. And it came to pass in those days, that she was sick, and died: whom when they had washed, they laid her in an upper chamber. And forasmuch as Lydda was nigh to Joppa, and the disciples had heard that Peter was there, they sent unto him two men, desiring him that he would not delay to come to them. Then Peter arose and went with them. When he was come, they brought him into the upper chamber: and all the widows stood by him weeping and shewing the coats and garments which Dorcas made while she was with them. But Peter put them all forth, and kneeled down, and prayed; and turning him to the body said, Tabitha, arise. And she opened her eyes: and when she saw Peter, she sat up. And he gave her his hand, and lifted her up, and when he had called the saints and widows,

presented her alive. And it was known throughout all Joppa; and many believed in the Lord.

Acts 9:36-42

Dorcas (Tabitha) is the only woman mentioned in the Bible as a disciple. We can see throughout the New Testament that Jesus' disciples were motivated toward people. Verse 36 tells us Dorcas was "full of good works and almsdeeds." Dorcas abounded continually in the work of the Lord with acts of kindness and charity. Dorcas had the gift of grace of giving which motivated her to meet the needs and wants of those around her. We can see this in verse 39 where it says all of the widows showed Peter coats and garments which she had made for them. Dorcas had quite an impact on the town of Joppa. Joppa was a major seaport 34 miles from Jerusalem. It was a large town considering it was not only Jerusalem's seaport but also the province of Judea's chief seaport. The majority of Joppa's men were in the hazardous profession of sailing, leaving many widows and orphans.

Dorcas met the needs of these widows. Dorcas was consistent in her giving, as verse 39 says every widow of Joppa had something to show Peter that was made by her. Peter was moved and impressed when he saw the widows at her bedside mourning the loss of their friend.

Dorcas was a living vessel of honor that poured forth God's love to those women; for she not only met their needs but she became their devoted and cherished friend. Dorcas utilized her God-given talents and abilities to become one of the greatest biblical examples of a giver.

Dorcas gave of her material possessions because it takes money to buy material to sew coats and garments. We also know she gave of her time because sewing coats and garments takes a lot of time, especially since she did it for every widow in the town of Joppa. Proverbs 31:20, in describing a virtuous woman, says: "She stretcheth out her hand to the poor; yea, she reacheth forth her hands to the needy." Dorcas' ability to be a servant to the widows in Joppa was because of the gift of grace of giving that was working through her accomplishing God's will for her life. Givers move toward people to meet their needs.

Pure religion and undefiled before God and the Father is this, To visit the fatherless and widows in their affliction, and to keep himself unspotted from the world.

James 1:27

Dorcas' religion was displayed through the love and care given to meet the needs of the widows and their families at Joppa.

CHARACTERISTICS OF THE GIFT OF GRACE OF GIVING IN REVIEW

The person with the gift of grace of giving:

1. Is motivated to support the saints in the body of Christ (Romans 12:8; definition of "giving").

2. Has a desire to impart spiritual gifts so the body of Christ will become established (Romans 1:11).

3. Is willing to share himself, his time and money for the work of the Lord (2 Corinthians 8:5; Acts 9:36; Luke 3:11).

4. Works well with his hands in order to help others in the body of Christ (Ephesians 4:28; Acts 9:39).

5. Looks past his circumstances and continues to give cheerfully in tithes, offerings, and almsdeeds (Acts 9:36; 2 Corinthians 8:2; Mark 12:41-44).

6. Has a readiness to give (2 Corinthians 8:11, 12, 19).

7. Is fulfilled when aiding and supporting the saints in the body of Christ (2 Corinthians 8:11, 12, 19).

8. Is motivated to give cheerfully out of a purposeful and determined heart (2 Corinthians 9:6-8).

9. Renders a service that supplies the needs and wants of the saints in the body of Christ (2 Corinthians 9:11, 12).

10. Is a catalyst for growth in prompting others in the body of Christ to be cheerful prompt-to-do givers (2 Corinthians 9:2).

God is the giver and He lives inside of you. The gift of grace of giving is an extension of the Father God teaching Christians how to give of their lives, time and money for the work of the Lord.

9

THE GIFT OF GRACE OF RULING (ORGANIZATION)

...he that ruleth, with diligence...

Romans 12:8

"**R**uleth," in the Greek, is *proistemi*, literally defined "to stand before, lead, and attend to." People with the gift of grace of ruling have the ability to organize, preside, oversee and maintain the body of Christ. Therefore, we can call the person with the gift of grace of ruling an organizer. God has given the gift of grace of ruling to the body of Christ to facilitate God's goals and objectives. An organizer is a person who promotes the ease of an action and the operation of it. The organizer is the maintenance part of the body of Christ.

And let ours also learn to maintain good works for necessary uses, that they be not unfruitful.

Titus 3:14

"Maintain" as used here in the Greek is also *proistemi,* the same word used in Romans 12:8 for "ruleth". We can see from this scripture that the organizer motivates the body of Christ to maintain good works. Let's look at this verse in the Amplified Bible.

And let our own (people really) learn to apply themselves to good deeds (to honest labor and honorable employment) so that they may be able to meet necessary demands whenever the occasion may require and not be living idle and uncultivated and unfruitful lives.

Organizers prevent the body of Christ from becoming idle and living unfruitful or unproductive lives. People with the gift of grace of ruling help the body of Christ define and carry out God's goals and objectives by delegating responsibility. An organizer sets goals and delegates responsibilities by lining people up to accomplish them.

This is a faithful saying, and these things I will that thou affirm constantly, that they which have believed in God might be careful to maintain good works. These things are good and profitable unto men.

Titus 3:8

"Maintain" used here, in the Greek, is also *proistemi.* We saw in the preceding scripture that the organizer is the maintenance part of the body of Christ. This scripture tells us when the body of Christ maintains good works, it becomes good and profitable for men. this shows us the importance of this gift to the body of Christ.

Organizers are willing to give of themselves to motivate others in the body of Christ to do the Lord's work. The gift of grace of ruling has been given to the body of Christ to cause believers to lead fruitful lives.

> **Herein is my Father glorified, that ye bear much fruit; so shall ye be my disciples.**
>
> **John 15:8**

A disciple of Christ bears fruit. "Fruit" used here, in the Greek, is *karpos* meaning the visible expression of power working inwardly; the character of the fruit being evidence of the power producing it. This definition simply means that fruit is the outward manifestation of the believers' inward convictions. People with the gift of grace of ruling cause the body of Christ to utilize their talents and abilities toward good works with fruit-bearing results.

In Titus 1:5, we see Paul leaving Titus in Crete to maintain the church as an organizer.

> **For this cause left I thee in Crete, that thou shouldest set in order the things that are wanting, and ordain elders in every city, as I had appointed thee.**
>
> **Titus 1 :5**

Titus had the gift of grace of ruling which motivated Paul to put him in charge of organizing churches in Crete and ordaining elders in every city assigned to him. Organizers, as we've studied, have the ability to delegate responsibility. Notice Paul told Titus to set in order the things that are lacking. Let's look at this verse in the Amplified Bible.

For this reason I left you (behind) in Crete, that you might set right what was defective and finish what was left undone, and that you might appoint elders and set them over the churches (assemblies) in every city as I directed you.

The first thing to note in the Amplified version is Paul's comment "I directed you." People with the gift of grace of ruling are under authority. Sometimes the gift of grace of ruling is misunderstood because it gives the connotation of power or supreme authority. This is untrue as typified by Titus carrying out Paul's instructions. People with the gift of grace of ruling have a desire to build upon the organized structure in the church.

Paul said Titus had the ability to see what was defective and unfinished in the body of Christ and set it right. Many Christians are inactive or wrongly placed in the body of Christ, causing defects or voids. People with the gift of grace of ruling have the ability to discern defects and/or voids in the body of Christ and remedy the situation. Titus' ability to discern defects and fill voids was because of the gift of grace of ruling working through him by God's supernatural power.

Organizers have the ability to see what is not functioning properly or what is needed in the body of Christ. They also have the ability to see God's goals and objectives that are being missed by the body of Christ.

They profess that they know God; but in works they deny him, being abominable, and disobedient, and unto every good work reprobate.

Titus 1:16

We saw earlier in Titus 3: 14 that people with the gift of grace of ruling motivate the body of Christ to do good works. Paul says some Christians deny God by their works. Organizers are given to the body of Christ to motivate the believers to accomplish God's goals that have been overlooked or ignored. The gift of grace of ruling is a two-fold blessing to the body of Christ for it not only defines God's goals and objectives, but also causes the body of Christ to accomplish them.

Organizers are grieved when the goals of God are not met. Notice it said in Titus 1:5, "and finish what was undone." Numerous procrastinators start out to accomplish God's goals but are easily distracted. This is not the case for individuals with the gift of grace of ruling. They see to it that God's goals are defined and completed as swiftly as possible. Let's look at some more characteristics of the gift of grace of ruling as defined in the Word of God.

For a bishop must be blameless, as the steward of God; not selfwilled, not soon angry, not given to wine, no striker, not given to filthy lucre.

Titus 1:7.

"Bishop" is *episkopos* in the Greek meaning one who is put in charge, overseer, or superintendent similar to the definition of ruling as one who presides and oversees. The ministry of a bishop and the gift of grace of ruling have similar characteristics. Consequently, the requirements of a bishop, as told by Paul, are similar to the characteristics of an organizer. "Blameless" means irreproachable in the Greek context. Christians put in positions of authority are required by God to have their lives beyond reproach. A person accepting a position of authority in the body of Christ becomes a representative of Jesus Christ, resulting in every aspect of his life being open for observation.

In all things shewing thyself a pattern of good works: in doctrine shewing uncorruptness, gravity, sincerity, sound speech, that cannot be condemned; that he that is of the contrary part may be ashamed, having no evil thing to say of you.

Titus 2:7, 8

Living an irreproachable life prevents Satan from getting in the door and destroying your reputation. People with the gift of grace of ruling are motivated to show a pattern of good works in their own life. An organizer does not have to be coerced into working for the Kingdom of God because he grieves when the goals of God are not completed.

Paul says overseers cannot be self-willed (carnal minded). "Self-willed," in the Greek, is *authodes* denoting one who is dominated by self-interest, and inconsiderate of others. People with the gift of grace of ruling have God's goals and objectives set before their eyes and are motivated by God to do His will. They are "not soon angry," meaning they are "slow to anger." People with the gift of grace of ruling are slow to anger in their labor among believers. When dealing with people the person with the gift of grace of ruling is not easily provoked and willing to endure negative reactions from people to accomplish God's ultimate objectives.

> **And show your own self in all respects to be a pattern and a model of good deeds and works, teaching what is unadulterated, showing gravity, having the strictest regard for truth and purity of motive, with dignity and seriousness. And let your instruction be sound and fit and wise and wholesome, vigorous and irrefutable and above censure, so that the opponent may be put to shame, finding nothing discrediting or evil to say about us.**
>
> **Titus 2:7, 8 Amplified Bible**

Notice in verse 7 it tells us, "show your own self in all respects to be a pattern and a model of good deeds and works." The gift of grace of teaching uses a scriptural pattern to mold believers so they fit into the Word of God. The person with the gift of grace of ruling uses his own life as a Godly pattern (example) to teach the body of Christ how to fit into God's plan. Other Christians cannot discredit the organizer because he uses his life to exemplify God's pattern.

Organizers aspire to see God's people working together in accomplishing God's objectives and are personally fulfilled upon the completion of His goals. They are interested in what will profit the body of Christ and further the Kingdom of God.

> **But a lover of hospitality, a lover of good men, sober, just, holy, temperate.**
>
> **Titus 1 :8**

Overseers are to be lovers of hospitality. "Hospitality" is philox-enes in the Greek, derived from the word *philos*, which means friendly. People with the gift of grace of ruling have the God-given ability to be sociable, gracious, and hospitable. Organizers consistently deal with people and are in a position to delegate responsibility through-out the body of Christ. This necessitates that they be friendly and harmonious.

Verse 8 continues by telling us an overseer is to be a lover of good people, sober minded, just and temperate. In this verse, "lover" and "good" are the same in the Greek, meaning a promoter of virtue and/or loving what is good. Organizers enjoy assembling themselves together to fellowship with other Christians. They are sober minded concerning God's program. The last characteristic of the person with the gift of grace of ruling as found in Titus 1:8, is they are just and upright. Not only are organizers just and upright but they also have the ability to discern these qualities in others. People with the gift of grace of ruling have the ability to discern and judge a person's capabilities.

Nehemiah had the gift of grace of ruling. Nehemiah 7:1 in the Amplified Bible shows this capability exemplified through his life.

> **Now when the wall was built, and I had set up the doors, and the gatekeepers, singers, and Levites had been appointed....**

Nehemiah's ability stemmed from his organizational gift of grace working through him discerning and placing the Levites and singers where they belonged in the House of God.

Holding fast the faithful word as he hath been taught, that he may be able by sound doctrine both to exhort and to convince the gainsayers.

Titus 1:9

The person with the gift of grace of ruling is unmoved by circumstances and is able to hold fast to keeping God's goals before his eyes and the believer's eye. People with the gift of grace of ruling hold fast to God's Word because they have the ability to give instruction through exhortation, motivating believers to act on it. The organizer also has the ability to reprove and convict those who oppose God's goals by showing them their error.

Let's look at the characteristics of the gift of grace of ruling in the life of Nehemiah.

NEHEMIAH:

Nehemiah, whose name means "consolation of God," had the gift of grace of ruling. We saw in the characteristics of ruling that this gift motivates believers toward accomplishing God's goals. Let's look at Nehemiah's life and see how those characteristics motivated him to complete God's goals.

And they said unto me, The remnant that are left of the captivity there in the province are in great affliction and reproach: the wall of Jerusalem also is broken down, and the gates thereof are burned with fire. And it came to pass, when I (Nehemiah) heard these words, that I sat down and wept, and mourned

certain days, and fasted, and prayed before the God of heaven.

Nehemiah 1:3, 4 (explanation mine)

Nehemiah had a concern for God's people as we can see by his intercession for the nation of Israel. Nehemiah was a cupbearer to King Artaxerxes Longimanus and even while living comfortably in that position, he had a concern and zeal for God's people in Jerusalem. People with the gift of grace of ruling have a concern and zeal for God's people. Their concern stems from their desire to see individuals work for God.

And the king said unto me, (the queen also sitting by him,) For how long shall thy journey be? and when wilt thou return? So it pleased the king to send me; and I set him a time.

Nehemiah 2:6

Notice it says Nehemiah set the time limit for the completion of the rebuilding of the walls of Jerusalem. People with the gift of grace of ruling have the ability to discern long range goals and set time limits on completion. Organizers are not procrastinators but are motivated to promptly accomplish God's goals.

Moreover I said unto the king, If it please the king, let letters be given me to the governors beyond the river, that they may convey me over till I come into Judah; And a letter unto Asaph the keeper of the king's forest, that he may give me timber to make beams for the gates of the palace which appertained to the house, and for the wall of the city, and for the

> **house that I shall enter into. And the king granted
> me, according to the good hand of my God upon
> me. Then I came to the governors beyond the river,
> and gave them the king's letters. Now the king had
> sent captains of the Army and horsemen with me.**
>
> **Nehemiah 2:7-9**

Nehemiah had the ability to see the overall picture, as shown by his conversation with the king. He systematically listed his supply requests as they would be needed. Nehemiah was aware of the resources that were available to him in repairing the walls and gates of Jerusalem. People with the gift of grace of ruling have the ability to see the overall picture and have awareness of the resources available to accomplish the task.

> **Then said I unto them, Ye see the distress that we are
> in, how Jerusalem lieth waste, and the gates thereof
> are burned with fire: come, and let us build up the
> wall of Jerusalem, that we be no more a reproach.
> Then I told them of the hand of my God which was
> good upon me; as also the king's words that he had
> spoken unto me. And they said, Let us rise up and
> build. So they strengthened their hands for this
> good work.**
>
> **Nehemiah 2:17, 18**

Nehemiah made it clear that Jerusalem was disgraced because of its deteriorated condition. We can see his strategy as he exhorts the Jews to act on his instructions from God. People with the gift of grace of ruling are fulfilled upon seeing the body of Christ come together in meeting God's goals. Nehemiah motivated the Jews by exhorting them with God's Word to accomplish the task of rebuilding the walls and gates. This is a major difference between a person with the gift of grace of ruling and a person with the gift of grace of serving. Servers like to work on the project themselves whereas organizers are motivated to bring believers together to accomplish the task. This does not mean organizers do not participate in the work, but rather they are primarily motivated toward team work.

Chapter 3 of Nehemiah shows him organizing Jewish workers for their individual gate assignments. It is noteworthy that Nehemiah assigned everyone to the gate closest to where they lived. An organizer has the ability to make the optimum use of the workers' time to organize people and place them in the most effective positions to accomplish the work of the Lord.

> **But it came to pass, that when Sanballat, and Tobiah, and the Arabians, and the Ammonites, and the Ashdodites, heard that the walls of Jerusalem were made up, that the breaches began to be stopped, then they were very wroth, And conspired all of them together to come and to fight against Jerusalem, and to hinder it. Nevertheless we made our prayer unto our God, and set a watch against them day and night, because of them.**
>
> **Nehemiah 4:7-9**

Nehemiah led the Jews in a prayer and then set a 24- hour watch for possible enemy attacks. Notice, Nehemiah was not concerned for he prayed, established a plan of defense and then continued with the task at hand. People with the gift of grace of ruling have the ability to keep God's goals in front of them even in the midst of adverse circumstances. We see that although other problems arose with the enemy in Nehemiah 4:12 and 21, it did not detour Nehemiah from the goal set before him.

> **And there was a great cry of the people and of their wives against their brethren and the Jews. For there were that said, We, our sons, and our daughters, are many: therefore we take up corn for them, that we may eat, and live. Some also there were that said, We have mortgaged our lands, vineyards, and houses, that we might buy corn, because of the dearth. There were also that said, We have borrowed money for the king's tribute, and that upon our lands and vineyards. Yet now our flesh is as the flesh of our brethren, our children as their children: and, lo, we bring into bondage our sons and our daughters to be servants, and some of our daughters are brought unto bondage already: neither is it in our power to redeem them; for other men have our lands and vineyards.**
>
> **Nehemiah 5:1-5**

The Jews became upset because they were having to sell their children to pay off loans. They were borrowing from their own people so they could continue to work on rebuilding the walls and gates of Jerusalem. Notice, they took out loans from their own people, not another tribe. Nehemiah's response in verse 7 was: "Then I consulted with myself, and I rebuked... them." We saw earlier in this chapter that the organizer has the ability to reprove and convict those who oppose God's goal, showing them to be in error. Verse 7 says Nehemiah consulted with himself and didn't form a committee nor did he line up both sides for a debate. Nehemiah had God's ability in him to solve this supposed stalemate. He dealt with the problem immediately (Nehemiah 5:11-13), saving time and loss of man hours. We can see that Nehemiah did not give up on God's goal (rebuilding the walls and gates for Jerusalem) but rather handled the brethren's problems as expeditiously as he handled pressure from the enemy.

In one of the definitions of ruling we find the word "organizer" means one who promotes the ease of an operation. Nehemiah was there to make things easier for those rebuilding the wall.

> **Moreover from the time that I was appointed to be their governor in the land of Judah, from the twentieth year even unto the two and thirtieth year of Artaxerxes the king, that is twelve years, I and my brethren have not eaten the bread of the governor. But the former governors that had been before me were chargeable unto the people, and had taken of them bread and wine, beside forty shekels of silver; yea, even their servants bare rule over the people: but so did not I, because of the fear of God.**
> **Yea, also I continued in the work of this wall, neither bought we any land: and all my servants were gathered thither unto the work. Moreover there were at my table a hundred and fifty of the Jews and rulers,**

beside those that came unto us from among the heathen that are about us. Now that which was prepared for me daily was one ox and six choice sheep; also fowls were prepared for me, and once in ten days store of all sorts of wine: yet for all this required not I the bread of the governor, because the bondage was heavy upon this people.

Nehemiah 5:14-18

Nehemiah knew his purpose was to make things easier and not become a burden on the Jews. People with the gift of grace of ruling have the ability to promote the ease and operation of a project. This gift of grace along with the others, aid and support the body of Christ. Notice in verse 19 Nehemiah says "according to all I have done for this people." Nehemiah lived a distance away yet cared enough for God's people to leave his plush job and return home to motivate the Jews to get back on their feet. The wall and gates were completed in 52 days showing that Nehemiah was a good steward of his time and manpower.

One of the last characteristics of the gift of grace of ruling displayed in the life of Nehemiah is the desire to organize and set things in order.

And God put into mine heart to gather together the nobles, and the rulers, and the people, that they might be reckoned by genealogy. And I found a register of the genealogy of them which came up at the first, and found written therein.

Nehemiah 7:5

Nehemiah had finished his project of rebuilding the walls and gates of Jerusalem. God put the desire in Nehemiah and gave him supernatural ability wherewith to organize the genealogical records of the Jews. People with the gift of grace of ruling have a desire to move on to new challenges in the body of Christ. Remember, the fulfillment of the organizer comes from bringing the body of Christ together to work on God's goals. Therefore, after one project is done he has a desire to move on to new challenges, thus preventing the body of Christ from being idle or fruitless.

CHARACTERISTICS OF THE GIFT OF GRACE OF RULING (ORGANIZATION) IN REVIEW

The person with the gift of grace of ruling (organization):

1. Has the ability to organize, preside, oversee, and maintain the body of Christ (Romans 12:8; definition of ruling).

2. Helps the body of Christ define and carry out God's goals and objectives by delegating responsibility (Titus 3:8,14; Nehemiah 2:17, 18).

3. Causes the body of Christ to utilize their talents and abilities toward good works (Titus 1:5; Nehemiah 1:3, 4).

4. Discerns defects and/or voids in the body of Christ and remedies the situation (Titus 1:5; Nehemiah 3:7).

5. Shows a pattern of good works in his own life as an example (Titus 2:7, 8; Nehemiah 5:14-19).

6. Has God's goals and objectives set before his eyes and is motivated to accomplish them (Titus 1:7).

7. Is slow to anger and willing to endure negative reactions from people in order to accomplish God's objective (Titus 1:7; Nehemiah 5:1-13).

8. Has the ability to be sociable, gracious, and hospitable (Titus 1:8)

9. Has the ability to discern and judge a person's capabilities (Titus 1:8; Nehemiah 7:1).

10. Holds fast to God's Word because he can give instructions through exhortation, motivating believers to act upon them (Titus 1:9).

11. Has a concern and zeal for God's people (Nehemiah 1:3, 4; Titus 1:8).

12. Discerns long-range goals and sets time limits on their completion (Nehemiah 2:6; 6:15).

13. Has the ability to discern the resources available to complete a project (Nehemiah 2:7, 8; Titus 1:5).

14. Has the ability to keep God's objectives in front of him even in the midst of adverse circumstances (Nehemiah 4:7-18, 21; 5:1-13).

15. Has the ability to promote ease and operation of a project (Nehemiah 5:14-19; 6:15).

16. Has a desire to move on to new challenges in the body of Christ preventing the body of Christ from living idle or fruitless lives (Nehemiah 5:14; 7:1-6).

The organizer is a desperately needed part of the body of Christ. God uses the gift of grace of ruling to set Christians in order and motivate them toward the Father's goals and objectives.

10

THE GIFT OF GRACE OF MERCY

...he that sheweth mercy, with cheerfulness.

Romans 12:8

The word "mercy" is *eleos* in the Greek and is defined as compassion that is active or compassion that leads to help. People with the gift of grace of mercy have compassion that leads to help. In order to understand the gift of grace of mercy, we need to compare the definition of mercy in the Hebrew and Greek. Mercy in the Hebrew is *kaphar* meaning to expiate or condone, to placate or cancel, cleanse, disannul, put off, and pardon. These definitions show us that mercy in Old Testament times dealt with pity, leaving no answer. Such pity resulted in temporary solutions like the mercy seat of God. A careful study of the mercy seat in the following scriptures will reveal that God's plan and purpose have always been to deal with mankind mercifully.

And thou shalt put the mercy seat above upon the ark; and in the ark thou shalt put the testimony that I shall give thee. And there I will meet with thee, and I will commune with thee from above the mercy seat, from between the two cherubims which are upon the ark of the testimony, of all things which I will give thee in commandment unto the children of Israel.

Exodus 25:21, 22

And when Moses was gone into the tabernacle of the congregation to speak with him, then he heard the voice of one speaking unto Him from off the mercy seat that was upon the ark of testimony, from between the two cherubims: and he spake unto him.

Numbers 7:89

And the LORD said unto Moses, Speak unto Aaron thy brother, that he come not at all times into the holy place within the veil before the mercy seat, which is upon the ark; that he die not: for I will appear in the cloud upon the mercy seat.

Leviticus 16:2

These scriptures signify God made His presence in the Old Testament known from the mercy seat. God's mercy covered the ordinances of the mosaic law, for He not only took care of the unlawful act, but also forgave the transgressor.

Jesus Christ is the mediator of a better covenant and He is our mercy seat as found in Hebrews 9:14, 15. Jesus Christ is the compassion that always leads to help. He is our witness from ever-lasting to everlasting of God's eternal mercy toward mankind.

In the Old Testament, God was continuously dealing with man's sins with the blood of bulls and goats, which was a temporary solution. In Leviticus chapter 16, two goats were used in the atonement ceremony (verse 7). Aaron was ordered to kill one of the goats for the sin offering (verse 15) and sprinkle the blood from that goat on the mercy seat. Notice it was the blood of the goat which made an atonement for the sins of the nation of Israel. The second goat (scapegoat) had the sins of the nation laid on it and then was set free into the wilderness, representing the taking away of the sins of the people.

God's Old Testament mercy extended beyond the law that was created to uncover the transgressor. Mercy took care of the offense and forgave the transgressor. God was able to show mercy to the children of Israel because of the blood of the sin offering of atonements which was offered once a year by a priest (Exodus 30:10). In Hebrews chapter 9, it tells us Jesus Christ, by His own blood has gone into the Holy of Holies and once and for all removed our sins. Jesus Christ is the High Priest and God's mercy seat full of compassion that leads to help.

The word mercy in the Hebrew, was not active, whereas in the Greek, "mercy" is active and leads to help. Mercy is compassion that leads to an action that meets the need of the individual.

But now hath he obtained a more excellent ministry, by how much also he is the mediator of a

better covenant, which was established upon better promises. For if that first covenant had been faultless, then should no place have been sought for the second.

Hebrews 8:6,7

Paul tells us the first covenant had faults, revealing God's reason for establishing a new covenant. Jesus Christ is our mediator who has made a way for mankind to be reconciled with the Father God with a better covenant (permanent solution for sin). God wanted reconciliation for His children once and for all, and His mercy extends toward all who will believe and accept Jesus Christ as the atonement for their sins.

All but one time in the New Testament we find the words "mercy" and "peace" together and in that order. Mercy is the compassionate act of God that leads to help, and peace is the resulting experience in the heart of man.

Many Christians have been confused in God's purpose for grace and mercy. Grace is an undeserved gift bestowed on a person. The Word of God tells us we are saved by grace.

For the grace of God that bringeth salvation hath appeared to all men.

Titus 2:11

Grace describes God's attitude toward sinners and rebellious Christians, whereas mercy is God's attitude toward those in distress (sick or needing help).

In review, "mercy" in the Hebrew had no action in response to the feeling of pity, whereas in the Greek, we find kindness and pity shown in compassion that leads to help (an answer). People with the gift of grace of mercy cannot separate their feelings of compassion from the action that meets an individual's need.

A common fallacy in the body of Christ is the belief that a person with the gift of grace of mercy feels pity toward others with no corresponding action. The truth is that mercy never separates the feeling of compassion or sympathy from the action to meet the need. The term "sloppy agape" cannot be applied to this gift, since this is a supernatural ability working through the believer. You might have heard the term sloppy agape used before, referring to a person with superficial love.

Let's see how the Word of God defines mercy:

> **And behold, two blind men sitting by the way side, when they heard that Jesus passed by, cried out, saying, Have mercy on us, O Lord, thou Son of David. And the multitude rebuked them, because they should hold their peace: but they cried the more, saying, Have mercy on us, O Lord, thou Son of David. And Jesus stood still, and called them, and said, What will ye that I shall do unto you? They say unto him, Lord, that our eyes may be opened. So Jesus had compassion on them, and touched their eyes: and immediately their eyes received sight, and they following him.**
>
> **Matthew 20:30-34**

"Mercy" used here in verses 30 and 31 is the same Greek word found in Romans 12:8. Notice, Jesus liked mercy with an action. When Jesus heard the men cry out for mercy, it says in verse 34 that He had compassion on them, revealing His pity and sympathy for them. Did it stop there? No, praise God. His compassion led to help as He healed the two blind men. The blind men asked Jesus for mercy knowing full well they were unworthy. Throughout the gospels, we find Jesus healing people because of a person's faith for He often commented, "Thy faith has made thee whole." These two men did not have that kind of faith. By their call for help, we can detect they had just heard that Jesus of Nazareth was passing by. The blind men called out for help the only way they knew how, by asking for mercy. They did not have the faith to receive healing. Jesus was not upset at their call for mercy and did not require any action of faith from them. It was an act of mercy (unmerited favor) that resulted in their healing.

Many Christians forget about God's mercy yet as we previously studied God deals with mankind from the mercy seat (Jesus Christ). The desire of God's heart is to deal with people through mercy. But the mercy of the Lord is from everlasting to everlasting upon them that fear him.

Psalms 103:17

"Compassion" is defined as suffering with another, sorrow for the distress or misfortunes of another, with the desire to help. Notice there is a desire to help even in the natural. God's gift of grace of mercy equips the believer with supernatural ability. The gift of grace

190

of mercy does not stop at the desire to help but continues resulting in help.

In the Greek, the word "compassion" is defined as "to be moved as to one's inwards." Compassion flows from one's emotions motivating them to help someone in distress. The two parts to mercy are compassion and help. Compassion moves in the inner being of a person with the gift of grace of mercy motivating him to meet the need of an individual in distress. The second part to mercy is the action that meets the need. We've studied that the gifts of grace are the energies of the Holy Spirit. God's energizing power produces unique effects. People with the gift of grace of mercy are motivated from their innermost being to help people who are in distress. It is God's energizing power working through them and motivating them toward people who need help. The person with the gift of grace of mercy gives people who are in distress an answer.

He shall call upon me, and I will answer him: I will be with him in trouble; I will deliver him, and honour him.

Psalm 91:15

This is God's answer for people who call upon Him when in trouble. We saw in the parable of the blind men that Jesus Christ was their answer. We're also told in Hebrews 4:16 to come boldly to the throne of grace and find mercy. When you are in trouble, it's not a time to run away from God; it is a time to run to Him and ask for mercy (His compassion that leads to help).

Let's look at another characteristic of the gift of grace of mercy. The Lord links forgiveness with mercy in Matthew 18:22-35.

Jesus saith unto him, I say not unto thee, Until seven times: but, Until seventy times seven. Therefore is the kingdom of heaven likened unto a certain king, which would take account of his servants. And when he had begun to reckon, one was brought unto him, which owed him ten thousand talents. But forasmuch as he had not to pay, his lord commanded him to be sold, and his wife, and children, and all that he had, and payment to be made. The servant therefore fell down, and worshiped him, saying, Lord, have patience with me, and I will pay thee all. Then the lord of that servant was moved with compassion, and loosed him, and forgave him the debt. But the same servant went out, and found one of his fellowservants, which owed him an hundred pence: and he laid hands on him, and took him by the throat, saying, Pay me that thou owest. And his fellowservant fell down at his feet, and besought him, saying, Have patience with me, and I will pay thee all. And he would not: but went and cast him into prison, till he should pay the debt. So when his fellowservants saw what was done, they were very sorry, and came and told unto their lord all that was done. Then his lord, after that he had called him, said unto him, O thou wicked servant, I forgave thee all that debt, because thou desiredst me: Shouldest not thou also

**have compassion on thy fellowservant, even as I had
pity on thee? And his lord was wrath, and delivered
him to the tormentors, till he should pay all that was
due unto him. So likewise shall my heavenly Father
do also unto you, if ye from your hearts forgive not
everyone his brother their trespasses.**

Matthew 18:22-35

The king represents the Lord Jesus Christ and the debt represents the sin of the world. Jesus Christ forgave and paid mankind's
debt of sin in full. Through Jesus Christ's death and resurrection
mankind was reconciled to the Father God. This parable shows us
King Jesus was willing to believe the best of His servant. People
with the gift of grace of mercy have the ability to believe the best of
a person. The king willingly believed the best of the servant, that he
would pay back the loan even though it was impossible. His compassion motivated Him to forgive and release the man from his debt.
The debt of man's sin could never be paid off without the sacrifice
of Jesus Christ. Compassion used here in verse 27 is the same word
as mercy in Romans 12:8. Compassion motivated the king's action
to forgive the debt. The king told his servant that he likewise should
have had the same compassion on his fellow servant instead of
putting the man in jail. Just as God in His infinite mercy pulled us
out of spiritual death and gave us eternal life through Jesus Christ,
we are expected to show similar mercy to mankind.

**But God, who is rich in mercy, for his great love
wherewith he loved us, Even when we were dead**

in sins hath quickened us together with Christ, (by grace ye are saved).

Ephesians 2:4-6

Paul tells us God is rich in mercy because of His great love for us. People with the gift of grace of mercy have the ability to extend great love toward people, regardless of their language or actions. People with the gift of grace of mercy have a supernatural ability to love people even if the person is in sin.

But love ye your enemies, and do good, and lend, hoping for nothing again: and your reward shall be great, and ye shall be the children of the Highest: for he is kind unto the unthankful and to the evil. Be ye therefore merciful, as your Father is also merciful.

Luke 6:35, 36

Verse 36 tells us "Be ye therefore merciful," linking the previous scripture to it. "Therefore" is a conjunction and it links the characteristics in verse 35 to mercy in verse 36. The first characteristic is to love our enemies just as our Father is merciful. People with the gift of grace of mercy have the ability to love their enemies. "Enemies" in the Greek is defined as an adversary or one that opposes you. After Jesus says to love our enemies, He goes on to tell us to do good. People with the gift of grace of mercy have the ability to do good toward people. Jesus said the world can love people who are loveable but the challenge is loving (showing mercy) to the unloveable. The Lord tells us we have the ability to love our enemies through His mercy working in us. Our ability extends far beyond the world's ability, for God has given us the ability to love, bless, pray and do good to our enemies. People with the gift of grace of mercy do not need to generate this response toward their enemies because it is a way of life for them.

> **And Jesus answering said, A certain man went down from Jerusalem to Jericho, and fell among thieves, which stripped him of his raiment, and wounded him, and departed, leaving him half dead. And by chance there came down a certain priest that way: and when he saw him, he passed by on the other side. And likewise a Levite, when he was at the place, came and looked on him, and passed by on the other side. But a certain Samaritan, as he journeyed, came where he was: and when he saw him, he had compassion on him, And went to him, and bound up his wounds, pouring in oil and wine, and set him on his own beast, and brought him to an inn, and took care of him. And on the morrow when he departed, he took out two pence, and gave them to the host, and said unto him, Take care of him; and whatsoever thou spendest more, when I come again, I will repay thee. Which now of these three, thinkest thou, was neighbour unto him that fell among the thieves? And he said, He that shewed mercy on him, Then said Jesus unto him, Go and do thou likewise.**
>
> **Luke 10:30-37**

Jesus tells us in this parable of the Good Samaritan how to show mercy. The man in verse 30 is Adam, representing mankind, whereas

Jerusalem represents heaven and Jericho represents earth. The thieves represent Satan, who stripped him of his raiment, wounded him, and departed, leaving him half dead representing spiritual death. The parable tells us a priest and Levite representing the law came by chance upon the man in need. The law was not designed to save man but to let him know of his sin and need for a savior. The Good Samaritan represents Jesus Christ and it tells us His journey was on purpose. Jesus Christ had a definite purpose in coming from Jerusalem (heaven) to Jericho (earth).

The Father God saw we were in trouble and sent His Son to remedy the situation. His compassion for us motivated Him to action. At the atoning work of Jesus Christ on the cross, He redeemed us from sin and sickness by pouring in two elements, oil and wine. The oil represents the oil of salvation and the wine represents the infilling of the Holy Spirit. Jesus ends the parable by telling us the Good Samaritan brought the man to an inn, which represents the church. The innkeeper is the Holy Spirit who has been entrusted to us for this dispensation until Jesus comes again. Jesus then asks the people which one of these three men was the neighbor. The lawyer answered, saying the neighbor was the Good Samaritan who showed mercy on the man. Jesus said go and do the same. Lift someone up out of despair and show him mercy by pointing them to Jesus Christ.

Ephesians 5:1 tells us to be imitators of God. The body of Christ is held accountable for more than their words.

And one of you say unto them, Depart in peace, be ye warmed and filled; notwithstanding ye give them

not those things which are needful to the body; what doth it profit?

James 2:16

People with the gift of grace of mercy show love in word and deed.

My little children, let us not love in word, neither in tongue; but in deed and truth.

1 John 3:18

John says the two parts to love are word and deed. Love speaks words of truth followed by the action that meets the need. These are God's key ingredients for mercy. Action is just as much a part of mercy as the feeling of compassion. People with the gift of grace of mercy always have an action that follows their words, causing the need to be met.

Let's look at a beautiful example of mercy in the New Testament. John was motivated by the gift of grace of mercy, as we can see in his writings to the body of Christ.

But whoso hath this world's good, and seeth his brothers have need, and shutteth up his bowel of compassion from him, how dwelleth the love of God in him?

1 John 3: 17

"Bowels" used here, in the Greek, is *splagchnon* meaning "the physical organs of the intestines" which signify the care and love felt in the innermost being of a believer toward those in need. John tells us compassion comes from inside the believer. John understood mercy because he was motivated by it and it became his way of life. From the deepest part of his inner being, the gift of grace of mercy caused him to love the unlovely and meet the needs of those in distress.

And this is his commandment, That we should believe on the name of his Son Jesus Christ, and love one another, as he gave us commandment.

1 John 3:23

This verse tells us walking in love is a commandment and is the key ingredient to living a life pleasing to God. John was motivated by the gift of grace of mercy which permeated through his writings in 1, 2 and 3 John, the Gospel of John, and the book of Revelation.

Jesus cared for all of His disciples but there was a special love and friendship between Jesus and John. John refers to himself as the disciple whom Jesus loved (John 19:26), revealing their special relationship. Shortly before His death on the cross, Jesus entrusted the care of His mother to John. John lived sixty years after the death of Jesus, during which time he continued to grow in his close and intimate relationship with Jesus as shown in the book of Revelation. The gift of grace of mercy working through John enabled him to write an abundance of revelation knowledge on love.

CHARACTERISTICS OF THE GIFT
OF GRACE OF MERCY IN REVIEW

The person with the gift of grace of mercy:

1. Has compassion that leads to help (Romans 12:8; definition of mercy).

2. Cannot separate his feelings of compassion from the action that meets the individual's need (Matthew 20:30-34; Psalm 91:15).

3. Has the ability to believe the best of people (Matthew 18:22-35).

4. Has the ability to extend great love toward people (Ephesians 2:4-6; 1 John 4:7, 11, 12).

5. Has the ability to love his enemies (Luke 6:35,36).

6. Has the ability to do good toward people (Luke 6:35,36).

7. Exemplifies love in two parts: word and deed (James 2:16; 1 John 3:16- 18; 4:20, 21).

Mercy is needed in the body of Christ along with the other gifts of grace. Love is exemplified through the gift of grace of mercy. God the Father expects all believers to show mercy because of the forgiveness and love He displayed to mankind in the death of His Son Jesus Christ. Through Jesus' death, mankind was reconciled to the Father God. Love never fails.

11

HOW TO FIND
YOUR GIFT OF GRACE

For I say, through the grace given unto me, to every man that is among you...

Romans 12:3

Having then gifts differing according to the grace that is given to us.

Romans 12:6

Paul says there is a grace given to every believer, and that grace will determine what ministry office(s) you receive. Your gift of grace will motivate you toward your ministry office(s) in the body of Christ.

We studied in chapter 3 how the believer is responsible for operating in all seven of the gifts of grace but is motivated by only one. For example, if you have the gift of grace of mercy and are operating in prophecy, you will still come from the merciful side of God. The gifts of grace are the unique energizings of the Holy Spirit working through believers causing the desire and power to concentrate on a particular spiritual concern.

A common misunderstanding is how many gifts of grace each believer receives. Each believer receives one gift of grace at the time of his spiritual birth. We know this from Paul's comment in Romans 12:4: "...all members have not the same office." Office is singular, not plural. Believers receive one gift of grace but are required to operate in all seven gifts of grace as illustrated in Scripture in the lives of Jesus, Peter, and Paul.

However, there are no limits regarding ministry gifts and manifestation gifts. As we can see in Paul's life, he received the following ministry offices as the Holy Spirit directed:

1. APOSTLE (1 Corinthians 1:1, 2; 2 Timothy 1:11)

2. TEACHER (2 Timothy 1:1 l; Acts 13:1; 1 Corinthians 4:17)

3. PROPHET (Acts 13:1)

4. PREACHER (2 Timothy 1:11)

5. EVANGELIST (Acts 15:40, 41)

Paul operated in all of the five-fold ministry offices and illustrations in chapter 3 showed him operating in all of the gifts of grace; yet he was motivated by the gift of grace, of prophecy. We also have confirmation of Paul functioning in all of the manifestations of the Holy Spirit throughout his ministry as the Holy Spirit directed.

The ministry offices are confirmed through the church while the manifestation gifts are directed by the Holy Spirit to profit all the believers.

ONLY YOU KNOW YOUR GIFT OF GRACE

The first thing you need to understand is that other people cannot find your gift of grace. They can see your outward actions and responses; however, they cannot be sure of your inward motivation. What others see in your outward behavior could be a result of training from childhood. For example, my parents entertained often during my childhood and taught me to be a good hostess. When I became a Christian, many believers recognized these talents and placed me in the church as a greeter and overseer of social functions. I love people and enjoy parties; however, I found out quickly that it was not my place since my joy was lost and the tasks became drudgery. After countless baby showers and socials, I informed my pastor's wife that this was not my ministry. She immediately responded that I had missed God because I was a natural at organizing social functions and getting along with people. She was right about me being a natural, but incorrect in that God's gifts (gifts of grace, ministry offices, manifestations of the Holy Spirit) are supernatural and not natural. As believers, we have to think spiritually. Everyone has been trained in certain areas which are not necessarily where God has placed them.

I had been diligently seeking God during my period of frustration as a greeter and organizer of church social functions. It became apparent that God had called me as a teacher, which gave me personal joy and fulfillment. Through the years, God has been continually developing this supernatural gift within me. I continue to entertain and even organize some social functions, although now I realize this is a natural gift. My true spiritual fulfillment, joy, and peace come from my supernatural gift of grace and office as a teacher. Remember, only you can know your gift of grace.

To identify your gift, you must look for joy in your heart when operating in your gift of grace. God will not give you a gift that causes personal dissatisfaction. There is a lady acquaintance of mine who used to get furious when anyone called her a server. She told me that she hated serving, yet was always serving those around her. One day I pulled her aside and told her if she would find out her gift of grace, she could start appreciating the gift of serving. To this day she is still miserable, struggling in her own fleshly efforts, not knowing her gift of grace.

TAKE THE PERSONAL PROFILE AND KNOW

Your first step in finding your gift of grace should be to take the personal profile found in chapter 12 of this book. After totaling your score, start to move out and focus your efforts in the direction of the highest total. In case of a tie, step out in both gifts of grace seeing which one brings you the most joy. Remember, not even your pastor can tell you what your gift of grace is, so do not let anyone rob you and God by placing you in the wrong position. God has placed the members in the body as it pleases Him. There are a lot of well-meaning Christians causing problems in the body of Christ by placing believers in the body as it pleases them. The sad repercussions of this practice are the detrimental effects on the believer and all those around them. The believer is unfulfilled and discouraged with a loss of joy. The general result is a sense of failure and feeling of uselessness toward the work of God.

> **As many as are led by the Spirit of God, they are called the sons of God.**
>
> **Romans 8:14**

Notice it does not say as many as are led by their pastor, spiritual leaders, friends, and parents are called the sons of God. However, you could receive a word (1 Corinthians 12:7,8) from another Christian which CONFIRMS what is already established in your spirit concerning your gift of grace.

The Spirit of God will lead and guide you to your place in the body of Christ. The first thing you need to do is get involved in a church. Remember, the ministry offices are confirmed through the church, while you are responsible for finding out your gift of grace which motivates you toward a ministry. God gives His spiritual gifts to profit the church and not just the believer. You will never fulfill God's plan for your life outside of the church. Stepping out in a church is your first responsibility. "For precept must be upon precept, precept upon precept; line upon line, line upon line; here a little, and there a little." Isaiah 28:10

Faith requires action. God cannot lead you unless you are moving so it is your responsibility to step out.

12

Gifts Of Grace Personal Profile

The purpose of this questionnaire is to help you discover your primary gift of grace in the body of Christ. This gift of grace personal profile is not a test. There are no "right" or "wrong" answers, and no one will ever see your results unless you choose to show them. Be as frank and honest as possible so that the questionnaire results give a true reflection of yourself.

Combining frequency of occurrence and degree of satisfaction, rate how true each statement is in your life by circling the appropriate number below each question.

0—Virtually never happens and/or produces dissastisfaction

1—Seldom happens and/or little satisfaction

2—Inconsistently happens and/or some satisfaction

3—Regularly happens and/or considerable satisfaction

4—Consistently happens and/or intense satisfaction

To receive an accurate interpretation of your gift of grace, you need to lean toward the joy and satisfaction you receive (unless otherwise instructed) when answering these questions. For example, one of the questions states, "If you are a guest at someone's home, would it be the norm to find yourself in the kitchen helping with the meal preparations whether you were specifically asked to do so? A lot of women have been trained from childhood that this is proper etiquette; therefore, their motive for serving originates from training and not because of the personal joy it brings. Remember these gifts are supernatural and bring personal joy, satisfaction and fulfillment. If you are always in the kitchen but it's not because you enjoy serving, then you would rate it 0 or 1, leaning toward a lack of satisfaction and not from the frequency of being in the kitchen. If you love to serve and thoroughly enjoy helping in the kitchen, circle 3 or 4 depending on the amount of joy, satisfaction, and fulfillment you receive.

This is a spiritual evaluation of your inner motivation and consequently, it is imperative for you to answer these questions honestly. When you finish answering the questions, turn to the pages immediately following the questions (How to Evaluate Your Gift of Grace Profile) for instructions on totaling your score.

PERSONAL PROFILE QUESTIONNAIRE

1. You express your opinion without considering other people's feelings.

    0 1 2 3 4

2. You are known for being reliable to get things done without constant supervision.

   0 1 2 3 4

3. You explain Biblical truths with explicit facts and details.

   0 1 2 3 4

4. You enjoy counselling believers.

   0 1 2 3 4

5. You have an ability to handle your finances with wisdom and frugality.

   0 1 2 3 4

6. You see effective results in recruiting people for projects or goals and have an ability to discern where people will be effective.

   0 1 2 3 4

7. You enjoy supporting and comforting a Christian who is suffering.

   0 1 2 3 4

8. You see everything as black or white, no grey or indefinite areas (rate this question on frequency of occurance).

   0 1 2 3 4

9. When working on a project, you go out of your way to make it special. For example, instead of buying blank name tags at the store, you would make them by hand.

   0 1 2 3 4

10 You are motivated to read the Bible and other reference books to gain in-depth knowledge.

0 1 2 3 4

11. You encourage others to develop in personal ministry (to do something for God).

0 1 2 3 4

12. You seek out special projects that need additional finances and resources.

0 1 2 3 4

13. You have the ability to work successfully with people by encouraging workers with approval, praise and challenges.

0 1 2 3 4

14. You have a tendency to attract people suffering from mental and emotional distress (rate this question on frequency of occurence).

0 1 2 3 4

15. You proclaim God's truth even when it's not well received (rate this question on frequency of occurence).

0 1 2 3 4

16. You view serving as the most important gift in the body of Christ.

0 1 2 3 4

17. You put an emphasis on the accuracy of factual data and words (rate this question on frequency of occurence).

    0 1 2 3 4

18. You have an inner motivation to explain Biblical truths with logical reasoning in order to make them accepted.

    0 1 2 3 4

19. You want to feel a part of the ministry to which you have financially and/or physically contributed.

    0 1 2 3 4

20. You have an ability to discern what responsibilities should or should not be delegated to others

    0 1 2 3 4

21. You take action to remove hurts and relieve distress in others.

    0 1 2 3 4

22. You have a desire to see outward signs of repentance displayed through the believer's inward conviction of sin (rate this question on frequency of occurence).

    0 1 2 3 4

23. You have an ability to discern and meet the practical needs of those around you.

    0 1 2 3 4

24. You have a need to validate truth and certify Biblical statements that have been made by others (rate this question on frequency of occurence).

    0 1 2 3 4

25. When counseling, you have an ability to visualize people's spiritual level and give steps of action to urge them toward spiritual maturity.

    0 1 2 3 4

26. You have a desire to motivate others to give of themselves, their time and money to the work of the Lord.

    0 1 2 3 4

27. You find yourself encouraging others to set goals (rate this question on frequency of occurence).

    0 1 2 3 4

28. You avoid conflicts and confrontations (rate this question on frequency of occurence).

    0 1 2 3 4

29. Wrong motives are easily discerned by you (rate this question on frequency of occurence).

    0 1 2 3 4

30. You are supportive of others who are in leadership.

    0 1 2 3 4

31. You assimilate information from several sources to find the answer to a question (rate this question on frequency of occurence).

    0 1 2 3 4

32. You are bothered when people have problems in their relationships (rate this question on frequency of occurence).

    0 1 2 3 4

33. You are motivated by the Lord's prompting and not at man's appeals to give as unto the Lord, whether it be money, time or yourself.

    0 1 2 3 4

34. You provide workable solutions to the problems facing a group or project.

    0 1 2 3 4

35. You have a tremendous capacity to show love to the seemingly unlovable.

    0 1 2 3 4

36. Even if the majority of people take a more tolerant position, you would boldly speak up against evil (rate this question on frequency of occurrence.

    0 1 2 3 4

37. You have difficulty saying "no" which results in your being caught up in a variety of projects and involvements (rate this question on frequency of occurence).

    0 1 2 3 4

38. You love to do word studies.

    0 1 2 3 4

39. Your motive for speaking to others is for their strengthening, encouragement, and comfort.

    0 1 2 3 4

40. You have a desire to give gifts of high quality (your best).

    0 1 2 3 4

41. You are highly motivated to organize any part of the church, group or project.

    0 1 2 3 4

42. Your spirit grieves when anyone is in distress.

    0 1 2 3 4

43. You are quick to grieve with others over their sins (rate this question on frequency of occurence).

    0 1 2 3 4

44. You show love for others through deeds and actions rather than words.

    0 1 2 3 4

45. You spend a lot of time reading the Bible.

    0 1 2 3 4

46. You restore confidence to the wavering and discouraged.

    0 1 2 3 4

47. You have a strong belief in tithing and in giving of offerings
    and almsdeeds.

    0 1 2 3 4

48. You enjoy working behind the scenes in order to promote the
    operation the smooth operation of a group or church.

    0 1 2 3 4

49. You close off your spirit to people whose words and actions
    reflect insensitivity to the feelings of others.

    0 1 2 3 4

50. Sometimes you have trouble separating the sin from the sinner.
    You find that you have bad feelings toward a person because of
    their sin (rate this question on frequency of occurence).

    0 1 2 3 4

51. Ladies:

    You are likely to be found in your hostesses' kitchens,
    helping with the meal preparations, whether or not you were
    specifically requested to do so (rate this question on joy and
    satisfaction).

    0 1 2 3 4

Men:

> If you went over to your friend's house for dinner and he was doing yard work, you would readily assist him to finish the task (rate this question on joy and satisfaction).
>
> 0 1 2 3 4

52. You tend to give extensive background details to validate a point or to display your research ability and knowledge.

    0 1 2 3 4

53. You prefer to witness with your life rather than verbally witnessing.

    0 1 2 3 4

54. You have a desire to give of yourself in quality time to doing things for the Lord.

    0 1 2 3 4

55. You enjoy all aspects of a project from small to large details.

    0 1 2 3 4

56. You can feel whether a group's atmosphere is joyful or in distress.

    0 1 2 3 4

57. You grieve in your spirit when any project or goal of God has been discontinued (rate this question on frequency of occurence).

    0 1 2 3 4

58. If there was a work day at the church, you would most likely be the first to arrive and the last to leave.

    0 1 2 3 4

59. You love to probe deep into the Bible for spiritual truths.

    0 1 2 3 4

60. You would evaluate yourself by saying you have an extra love for people in general.

    0 1 2 3 4

61. You dislike flamboyant giving.

    0 1 2 3 4

62. You are goal oriented. You would like to set goals that lead to the completion of a project.

    0 1 2 3 4

63. You rejoice to see others blessed and grieve when others are hurt.

    0 1 2 3 4

64. You are persuasive in your method of speaking when defining what is right or wrong.

    0 1 2 3 4

65. It would be very typical for you to use your personal funds for a project you were involved in at church, such as decorating for a special event, painting a classroom, etc..

    0 1 2 3 4

66. You easily spot and are bothered by scriptural illustrations presented out of context (rate this question on frequency of occurence).

    0 1 2 3 4

67. You have the ability to spot the problems of individuals and offer spiritual solutions as stepping stones for spiritual growth and victory in their lives.

    0 1 2 3 4

68. You spot the financial needs of those in Christian work (missions, evangelists, etc.) and bring those needs to the attention of others in a position to help.

    0 1 2 3 4

69. You are motivated to complete a given task without procrasination (rate this question on frequency of occurrence).

    0 1 2 3 4

70. You prefer the company of sensitive, personable, individuals.

    0 1 2 3 4

71. You expect immediate evidence of repentence after counseling someone (rate this question on frequency of occurence).

    0 1 2 3 4

72. You find yourself involved in so many activiates that your family is sometimes neglected (rate this question on frequency of occurence.

    0 1 2 3 4

73. You don't have any problem spending hours studying the Bible (rate this question on frequency of occurence).

0 1 2 3 4

74. You are bothered when truth is presented without practical application.

0 1 2 3 4

75. You believe God is your total source for meeting all your needs. For example, you have $10.00 left in your checkbook. You would have no problem giving it away as the Lord led because of your confidence in God as your source.

0 1 2 3 4

76. You are good at evaluating an individual's ability to perfrom a given task.

0 1 2 3 4

77. You avoid being firm with others unless you can see that it is clearly for their benefit.

0 1 2 3 4

78. You are extremely critical of yourself and grieve upon failing God (rate this question on frequency of occurence).

0 1 2 3 4

79. When doing a specific job, it is not unusual for you to get sidetracked by the strong immediate need of another.

0 1 2 3 4

80. You believe teaching is foundational to the operation of all other gifts.

    0 1 2 3 4

81. You accept people as they are without judging them.

    0 1 2 3 4

82. You are concerned where your money goes and keep informed on the projects or people you give to, making sure your gift is bearing fruit.

    0 1 2 3 4

83. You have the ability to know all the resources available to complete the task(s) you start.

    0 1 2 3 4

84. You find it difficult to have close fellowship with those who are insensitive (rate this question on frequency of occurence).

    0 1 2 3 4

85. You have strong convictions and strict personal standards (rate this question o frequency of occurence).

    0 1 2 3 4

86. You would rather complete a job yourself than delegate it to someone else.

    0 1 2 3 4

87. You enjoy sharing Biblical truths one on one.

    0 1 2 3 4

88. You find truth in experiences and then validate it with scriptures.

    0 1 2 3 4

89. You have no problem tithing from your first fruits (before taxes).

    0 1 2 3 4

90. Watching a project come together and people operating in their God-given gifts brings more satisfaction and joy than your personal accomplishment.

    0 1 2 3 4

91. At times you find yourself getting upset at the person who has had problems with the one you are counseling.

    0 1 2 3 4

92. You have a strong desire to be obedient to God at all costs.

    0 1 2 3 4

93. You are unfulfilled when not involved in church.

    0 1 2 3 4

94. You have a tendency to remain silent concerning Biblical teachings until information has been heard, analyzed and discussed.

    0 1 2 3 4

95. You see your trials as opportunities to produce spiritual growth.

    0 1 2 3 4

96. You do not have to be urged, coerced, or shamed into giving freely. You are not moved by the needs (rate the question on frequency of occurence).

    0 1 2 3 4

97. You will not give up on a project, even if it looks impossible. You stick it out until the project is completed.

    0 1 2 3 4

98. You have a need for deep friendships in which there is mutual commitment.

    0 1 2 3 4

HOW TO EVALUATE YOUR GIFT OF GRACE PROFILE

PROPHECY: This gift of grace is one which discerns the motives of others and is actively involved with restoring and repairing within the body.

You are able to look into the very soul and discern the inner motives of others. You should use this gift to encourage, exhort and comfort people. You abhor evil and are quick to point it out. You are deeply concerned about the spiritual condition of others and are frank and candid in dealing with those who are caught in sin. You love to see people get right with God and pray with people for salvation. You may appear impersonal, but you are a vital part of God's program.

It is easy to misjudge those with the gift of grace of prophecy as being insensitive to people's feelings or overly harsh regarding sin.

If you find yourself motivated by the gift of grace of prophecy, you need to develop this gift in love.

Total your score on questions 1, 8, 15, 22, 29, 36, 43, 50, 57, 64, 71, 78, 85, and 92.

MINISTRY: This gift of grace is a service in which one finds a desire and concern to meet the practical needs of the body of Christ.

You discern and meet the practical needs of the church. You exemplify the life and attitude of the Lord Jesus Christ who came to serve mankind. You have energy which enables you to get involved in many projects of service in the church. You love people and receive fulfillment when serving them.

Total your score on questions 2, 9, 16, 23, 30, 37, 44, 51, 58, 65, 72, 79, 86, and 93.

TEACHING: This gift of grace is one which motivates one to research. You have an ability to instruct, and explain truth by a form of doctrine that molds and shapes people in line with God's Word.

You love to read and study God's Word and delight in discovering new truths. You are motivated to reveal these truths by instructing individuals with scriptural patterns that shape them in line with God's truth.

If you find yourself motivated by the gift of grace of teaching, you need to realize the importance of spending time in the Word in order to expound on the things of God. It is imperative that the Bible is your final source.

Total your score on questions 3, 10, 17, 24, 31, 38, 45, 52, 59, 66, 73, 80, 87, and 94.

EXHORTATION: This gift of grace is one which stimulates faith by encouraging, consoling and comforting the body of Christ.

You are positive and encouraging in your love for others. You love to exhort the body of Christ on how to live a life pleasing to God. You are able to transmit your faith causing spiritual growth in a recipient's life.

If you find yourself motivated by the gift of grace of exhortation, you need to realize you are an expression of the Holy Spirit who is your guide on how to exhort, console, and comfort the body of Christ.

Total your score on questions 4, 11, 18, 25, 32, 39, 46, 53, 60, 67, 74, 81, 88, and 95.

GIVING: This gift of grace is embodied in one who gives of themselves, their time, and money as well as motivates others to give to the work of the Lord.

You have a desire to give without an emotional appeal or being coerced. You give quietly unless your gift is to be made public in order to motivate others to give. You are concerned that your giving bears fruit and so you keep informed on projects and people receiving your financial support.

If you find you are motivated by the gift of grace of giving, you need to realize you have the ability to spend (share and impart) your life with others.

Total your score on questions 5, 12, 19, 26, 33, 40, 47, 54, 61, 68, 75, 82, 89, and 96.

RULING: This gift of grace is one which motivates a person to organize in order to promote the smooth operation of a group or church.

You aid in the facilitation of the body of Christ by defining and carrying out God's goals and objectives. You have an ability to work with people successfully by encouraging workers with approval, praise and challenges. You receive more satisfaction and joy from watching a project come together and the body of Christ operating in their God-given gifts than in your own personal accomplishment.

If you find you are motivated by the gift of grace of ruling, you need to realize you are desperately needed in the maintenance part of the body of Christ.

Total your score on questions 6, 13, 20, 27, 34, 41, 48, 55, 62, 69, 76, 83, 90, and 97.

MERCY: This gift of grace enables one to identify with individuals' hurts and frustrations thereby motivating others to act compassionately like our Lord and Savior Jesus Christ.

You have an ability to discern and identify people with needs. You show love in word and deed. You close your spirit to people whose words and actions reflect insensitivity to the feelings of others. You have the ability to love your enemies and the unlovely.

If you find you are motivated by the gift of grace of mercy, you need to be careful you walk by faith, not by sight or feelings.

Total your score on questions 7, 14, 21, 28, 35, 42, 49, 56, 63, 70, 77, 84, 91, and 98.

Select your highest total from among the seven gifts of grace. If the questions on this personal profile have been answered honestly with an emphasis on joy and fulfillment, then the highest score should represent your gift of grace.

13

OPERATING IN
YOUR GIFTS AND CALLINGS

STEP OUT WITH JOY

So shall my word be that goeth forth out of my mouth: it shall not return unto me void, but it shall accomplish that which I please, and it shall prosper in the thing whereto I sent it. For ye shall go out with joy and be led forth with peace.

Isaiah 55:11, 12

God's will concerning your life as shown in Isaiah 55:11, 12 has two stipulations. The first requirement is to go out with joy. Your gift of grace and office(s) will bring you joy and fulfillment when operating in them. If you have stepped out and find your joy has turned into drudgery, STOP! This not only displeases you but also the Father God. Step out in another direction with joy, always remembering that in His presence there is "fullness of joy." When walking in God's perfect will, you are in His presence where there is fullness of joy. Do not go out without your joy, as that is like going out without God since He is your exceeding joy (Psalms 43:4).

Remember the initial joy upon becoming saved? David prayed: "Restore unto me the joy of thy salvation; and uphold me with thy free spirit" (Psalm 51:12). This is a good place to start if you have lost your joy. Pray that God would restore the joy of your salvation. David knew the freedom and exceeding joy of walking with God.

BE LED FORTH WITH PEACE

The second requirement to finding your gift of grace and office(s) is being led by peace (Isaiah 55:12). "Peace" is defined in the Hebrew as the state of being at ease as is experienced both externally and internally.

I will both lay me down in peace, and sleep: for thou, LORD, only makest me dwell in safety.

Psalm 4:8

Notice peace is external and internal dealing with your SPIRIT, SOUL, AND BODY. Throughout this book we have covered spiritual gifts as being supernatural ability, not fleshly efforts. There should be no struggling or striving regarding God's work.

Peace I leave with you, my peace I give unto you: not as the world giveth, give I unto you. Let not your heart be troubled, neither let it be afraid.

John 14:27

God's peace is a combination of harmony and wholeness as your spirit, soul, and body are at peace with one another. Be ruled by the Prince of Peace and not by circumstance. God's Word says to let His peace lead you. If your area of church involvement has disrupted your peace, then you need to stop, get before God, and listen for a new direction.

Be still and know that I am God...

Psalm 46:10

Hearing from God seems to be difficult for many Christians. One of the major keys is to be still. In this day and age, people have been trained to be fast and progressive.

The Word of God tells us man makes plans but the Lord directs his steps (Proverbs 16:9). Making plans is the first step prior to taking action.

For thou wilt light my candle: the Lord my God will enlighten my darkness.

Psalms 18:28

Make plans but let God light your pathway and direct your steps. God promises you that He will lead and guide you into all truth regarding His will for your life.

Lead me in thy truth, and teach me: for thou art the God of my salvation; on thee do I wait all the day.

Psalm 25:5

"Wait" used here, in the Hebrew, means to serve or wait on tables, having the connotation of action. David was a man of action always stepping out and moving in God's direction. When missing God he was quick to repent and head in another direction.

But they that wait upon the LORD shall renew their strength; they shall mount up with wings as eagles; they shall run, and not be weary; and they shall walk, and not faint.

Isaiah 40:31

"Wait" used here in Isaiah is the same word as "wait" used in Psalm 25:5. Most people incorrectly think that wait means to stand still. There are other aspects to waiting; for instance, it also means to patiently watch with expectation. While you are waiting to hear from God, be doing something to further His Kingdom. Step out and do something while you're waiting on God to direct your next step. Can you turn a car when it's parked? Of course not! God cannot force you to move when you're standing still. Remember: God's leading comes with peace.

Making plans should be in response to your gift of grace motivating you toward God's direction. Be assured that the Holy Spirit will lead and direct your steps one at a time (Isaiah 28:10).

As we studied earlier in the parable of the talents found in Matthew 25, Jesus said to the wicked and slothful servant that the least he could have done was to put the money in the bank to draw interest. Jesus is telling us likewise to do something now with our God-given talents and abilities.

USE IT OR LOSE IT:

For unto every one that hath shall be given, and he shall have abundance: but from him that hath not shall be taken away even that which he hath.

Matthew 25:29

We can glean from this scripture and parable that every Christian receives spiritual endowments and then is accountable. If he uses his God-given talents, abilities, and responsibilities, then more will be added to him.

Many Christians are confused with the portion of this scripture that states "...from him that hath not shall be taken away even that which he hath." This seems cruel, but this holds true likewise in the secular world. For example, my husband and I took several years of Spanish in high school. We have subsequently lost the ability to speak, write, and understand Spanish due to a lack of practice and use of this language.

This same principle occurs in God's Kingdom. The only difference is God will not allow any talent or ability to go to waste so He takes it away from the Christian who has buried it (failed to use it) and gives it to someone who will use it. Jesus took the talent from the wicked and slothful servant and gave it to the one who had multiplied his talents to ten (Matthew 25:29).

I am the true vine, and my Father is the husband-man. Every branch in me that beareth not fruit he

taketh away: and every branch that beareth fruit, he purgeth it, that it may bring forth more fruit.

John 15: 1, 2

This scripture is a confirmation of Matthew 25:29. Your sufficiency is of God since He equips you with everything needed to step out and use your spiritual endowments. Jesus tells us there are two requirements of a branch (Christian).

1.   It must be IN HIM (sufficiency is of God).

2.   It must BEAR FRUIT (productive life).

God's sufficiency is in the vine which is Jesus Christ. The phrase "in me" refers to Christians since you cannot be in Him (Jesus Christ) unless you are saved. This scripture further states that Jesus will purge the branch or Christian who is not bearing fruit. "Purge," in the Greek, means prune signifying that the non-producing areas of a Christian's life will be cut off. This is not in reference to salvation but refers to the productivity of a Christian. Pruning is cutting out the useless or undesirable parts which results in the remaining plant becoming healthier and increasing production of fruit. God will take away the aspects of your life that are not producing fruit.

A lot of you by now are probably concerned with losing your God-given spiritual talents and abilities. Let's look at a scripture that will clear up this question.

For the gifts and calling of God are without repentance.

Romans 11:29

"Gifts" used here, in the Greek, is *charisma* (gifts of grace Romans 12:6-8). Notice Paul states the gifts of grace and callings are without repentance. "Repentance," in the Greek, means "irrevocable" which tells us the gifts of grace cannot be taken back. One of the reasons for this is because the gifts of grace are God's motivating power directing Christians to their place (ministry office(s) in the body of Christ. God will not take back your gift of grace or His calling (ministry office) on your life. However, if you choose to bury your God-given endowments (supernatural talents and abilities), then and only then will God give them to other Christians who are willing to use them (Matthew 25:29).

Fruit is the evidence of a productive life for a Christian. In the Greek and also in English, "fruit" is defined as the useful product of a plant, tree, bush or vine. Although the Greek goes a step further in telling us how the fruit is brought forth: "to seize in various applications, to catch, pluck, pull or take by force." God expects the believer to bear fruit in a variety of ways.

Every Christian needs to evaluate all areas of his life to see if he is producing fruit. If you have areas not producing fruit, then you might be in the wrong position and need to ask God for new direction. When you find an area of your life that is producing fruit, allow God to prune it, resulting in a bumper crop.

EVERY JOINT SUPPLIETH

Every Christian is important to God and has a God given plan for his life.

From whom the whole body fitly joined together and compacted by that which every joint supplieth, according to the effectual working in the measure of every part, maketh increase of the body unto the edifying of itself in love.

Ephesians 4: 16

The "whole body" refers to the body of Christ made up of "joints" referring to the individual Christian. "Supplieth" is *epichoregia* in the Greek, meaning to fully nourish and/or contribute or minister. This scripture gives us the results of the whole body of Christ moving out in their ministry offices in Christ. Notice every joint is required to supply or contribute. Numbers 23: 19 tells us, "God is not a man that he should lie." The Word tells us that every joint (Christian) has something to contribute to the work of God.

After studying the Word, we have seen the truth about a Christian's responsibility concerning spiritual gifts. If you continue to take up the argument that God uses some Christians in the ministry and not others, then you are slandering the Word of God. Ephesians 4: 16 says every joint (Christian) is required to supply (nourish, aid, contritbute and minister).

As an analogy, let's look at the word "family" that encompasses a father, mother and children. If we take out the children, it becomes a couple, or if we remove the parents, the children become orphans. To be complete, every part has to be present. Likewise in the body of Christ if some of our parts are missing we have a void in certain areas resulting in overall weaknesses in the body. It is vital that Christians perceive God's vision for the church as shown in Ephesians 4:16 and as individuals, contribute their part to the body of Christ.

14

THE APPOINTMENT OF MINISTRY GIFTS IN THE CHURCH

There is a scriptural basis in the Word of God for how ministry gifts are appointed.

> Wherefore, brethren, look ye out among you seven
> men of honest report, full of the Holy Ghost and
> wisdom, whom ye may appoint over this business.
> But we will give ourselves continually to prayer, and
> to the ministry of the word. And the saying pleased
> the whole multitude: and they chose Stephen, a man
> full of faith and of the Holy Ghost, and Philip, and
> Prochorus, and Nicanor, and Timon, and Parme-
> nas, and Nicolas a proselyte of Antioch: whom they
> set before the apostles; and when they had prayed,
> they laid their hands on them.

And the Word of God increased; and the number of the disciples multiplied in Jerusalem greatly; and a great company of the priests were obedient to the faith.

Acts 6:3-7

The requirements for the appointment of ministry gifts in the church:

1. HONEST REPORT
2. FULL OF THE HOLY GHOST AND WISDOM
3. INTERVIEW
4. PRAYER
5. LAYING ON OF HANDS

HONEST REPORT

The first requirement Paul mentions in the appointment of ministry gifts in the church is to look out among them (body of Christ) for men of honest report. The usage of the word "men" does not limit ministry gifts (offices) to the male gender, for woman in the Hebrew means "man with a womb" therefore, men is in reference to both male and female. Ministry offices are confirmed in the church. In Acts 6, they were looking for Christians with a good reputation who were involved in the church. First Timothy 3:7 tells us "Moreover he, (a believer put in the ministry position of bishop) must have a good report of them which are without, lest he fall into reproach and the snare of the devil" (explanation mine). "Those who are without" refers to individuals in the secular world. The man who is appointed to a ministry position in the church must be in good standing in their community (both Christian and secular). To be of honest report you cannot be a novice since it take time to study to show yourself approved (2 Timothy 2:5). We studied the parable of the talents in Matthew and found Christians are required to be faithful over their few God-given talents and abilities and then they will become responsible for bigger things, indicating there is time involved in spiritual growth. This is explained in detail later in this chapter through the lives of Paul and Timothy. Paul warns us in 1 Timothy 3:6 that a novice can be lifted up with pride causing him to fall and receive condemnation of the devil. Colossians 2:7 tells us, "Rooted and built up in him, and established in the faith, as ye have been taught..." The believer has to be taught to be rooted, grounded, and established in the Word.

FULL OF THE HOLY GHOST AND WISDOM

The second requirement for a believer prior to being placed in a ministry office is to be full of the Holy Ghost and wisdom. The in-filling of the Holy Spirit is not a choice but a commandment from the Lord Jesus Christ to Christians.

> **And, being assembled together with them, commanded them that they should not depart from Jerusalem but wait for the promise of the Father, which saith he, ye have heard of me. For John truly baptized with water; but ye shall be baptized with the Holy Ghost not many days hence. When they therefore were come together, they asked of him,**

**saying, Lord, wilt thou at this time restore again
the kingdom to Israel? And he said unto them, It is
not for you to know the times or the seasons, which
the Father hath put in his own power. But ye shall
receive power after that the Holy Ghost is come
upon you and ye shall be witnesses unto me both in
Jerusalem, and in all Judaea, and in Samaria, and
unto the uttermost part of the earth.**

Acts 1:4-8

Jesus commanded them to wait for the infilling of the Holy
Spirit. It is imperative that Christians realize the power comes from
the fullness of the Holy Spirit. This is God's miracle working, inherent power that includes His ability, strength, and might which is
available to every believer through the infilling of the Holy Spirit.
Many Christians are working for God in their own power and
strength, which will not work since He never intended for believers
to do it in their own fleshly efforts. Our sufficiency is of God and
not man. You need to be filled with the Holy Spirit and power in
order for God to work most effectively through your ministry. Salvation and the infilling or baptism of the Holy Spirit are two separate
experiences. In Acts 6, Jesus' command to wait for the baptism of the
Holy Spirit was given to the Jews who had believed in Him. Salvation is a prerequisite for the infilling (baptism) of the Holy Spirit.

Notice in Acts 6:3 it says, "full of the Holy Ghost and wisdom."
"Wisdom" used here, in the Greek, is referring to insight and application into spiritual things. Wisdom is the correct application of
knowledge. Wisdom can only come from spending time in the Word

of God. The infilling of the Holy Spirit allows the wisdom of God to flow through you. God tells us the Holy Spirit has been given to lead and guide us into all wisdom and revelation knowledge. Jesus said, "Every plant, which my heavenly Father hath not planted shall be rooted up" (Matthew 15: 13). Wisdom comes from being rooted and grounded in the Word of God which is Jesus Christ.

INTERVIEW

The third requirement for the appointment of ministry gifts in the church is an interview between the spiritual leaders and the applicant. After the spiritual leaders chose the men with an honest report, full of the Holy Spirit and wisdom, then they set them before the apostles. "Set", in the Greek, means appointment referring to choosing for an office or position. For example, in the secular world a person applying for a job is required to appear at an interview. Likewise the apostles (spiritual leaders) interviewed the men before placing them in their ministry.

PRAYER

After the interview, the spiritual leaders prayed to receive confirmation from God on the placement of believers in their ministry office. The believer should be prayed over (Acts 6:6) upon being accepted for a ministry office. Prayer is a form of communication with the Father God and is a necessity when placing believers in their ministry office. Through prayer, the spiritual leaders receive confirmation from God on the placement of believers in their ministry office.

LAYING ON OF HANDS

The laying on of hands acknowledges a person who has been set apart for a specific work.

> **As they ministered to the Lord, and fasted, the Holy Ghost said, Separate me Barnabas and Saul for the work whereunto I have called them.**
>
> **Acts 13:2**

Notice the Holy Spirit said they were to separate themselves unto Him and the special work in which they had been called. "Ministered" used here, in the Greek, means worship, pray, and obey. Prayer over a believer called into a ministry position signifies a setting apart and an obedience to that calling.

Laying on of hands is the last requirement of appointment to ministry gifts in the church.

> **And when they had fasted and prayed, and laid their hands on them, they sent them away.**
>
> **Acts 13:3**

A believer interviewed and accepted for a position should be prayed over and have hands laid on them (Acts 6:6). We can see that prayer and laying on of hands are closely tied together. Laying on of hands by the apostles or elders in today's church acknowledges a member or members for particular work by setting them apart and giving evidence of the individual's having the necessary qualifications. For example, 1 Timothy 4:14 tells us that Timothy received the impartation of a spiritual gift through the laying on of hands by the presbyters. Timothy had the confirmation of this appointment already in his heart since God gives the individual believer revelation knowledge of his calling (anointing). God always uses the spiritual leaders of the church to confirm the believer's ministry office.

Acts 6:3 tells us that seven men of honest report were appointed over a business. Appointed as we saw earlier, is for the church's recognition of those who had already been raised up, qualified by the Holy Spirit, and given evidence of an honest report and wisdom. "Business" is *chreia* in the Greek meaning employment by requirement signifying that the above requirements must be met first for church employment. God sees the appointment of ministry gifts (offices) in the church as an employment.

The pendulum seems to swing in both radical directions concerning appointment of ministry gifts (office) in many of today's churches. One side is so unscriptural with appointments being given solely by the need with no necessary qualifications for the person filling the position except for availability, the least important qualification. God is not moved by needs. Many churches fill ministry offices by the need instead of the person's calling. For example, Sunday school teachers are in great demand in many churches with the unfortunate result being that many young Christians are placed in this position when they should be in the services hearing the Word of God. Many of these new Christians eventually get burned out, discouraged and sometimes end up dropping completely out of church. The body of Christ is responsible for the growth of new converts. Paul warns us in 1 Timothy 3:6 of the danger of putting a novice in such a position. Let's start using biblical principles in the placement of believers in the body of Christ.

The other side of the pendulum is super spiritual thinking, placing individuals with no interview or qualifications, solely on the basis that they "can do all things through Christ who strengthens" them. Both of these methods are wrong. Paul said in Romans 12:3 for believers to think soberly and/or realistically about their measure (position) in the church. Not everyone can be a pastor or evangelist, no matter how many times they confess, "I can do all things through Christ who strengthens me;" it is still God who distributes the spiritual endowments.

God knows who He has equipped for each position in the body of Christ and it is essential to use His requirements in the appointment of ministry offices. God's Church is a business and He expects the body of Christ to think soberly (realistically) about their ministry (position). Many Christians in the body of Christ are dreamers, thinking unrealistically about their measure. We know God has a plan for each one of our lives and that every joint (believer) is required to supply (operate in their ministry offices as stated in Ephesians 4:16 and 1 Corinthians 12:14-21. The eye cannot say to the ear he has no need of him. We need each other; that's why Jesus prayed that the body of Christ would perceive through their spiritual eyes that God's gifts are spiritual (supernatural ability and talent).

Now that we've seen God's method of placing believers in their ministry offices, let's look at some biblical examples of this process.

PAUL

Paul's gift of grace was prophecy, defined in chapter 3 as an inspired speaker who speaks forth the mind and counsel of God.

Honest Report:

Paul had a poor reputation after his conversion due to a past history of persecuting the Jews. The disciples had to secretly remove him from Damascus because of threats on his life. Acts 9:27 states Barnabas brought Paul before the apostles (leaders) in Jerusalem and spoke in his defense. The Bible says God will exalt us and He did so for Paul through Barnabas' testimony. The honest report about Paul came from Barnabas having a sound reputation among the Christians. Paul's ministry lasted two weeks in Jerusalem since the Greeks wanted to kill him, forcing him to flee to his birthplace at Tarsus. This begins an unrecorded ten year period in the life of Paul. Obviously, he studied and showed himself approved since Barnabas heard of his work and went to Tarsus to summon Paul to Antioch (Acts 11:25). They stayed one year in Antioch, teaching the disciples with Paul becoming Barnabas' prodigy. We can see by the sequence of events that Paul studied and showed himself an approved workman for God and a fellow laborer in the body of Christ. At the beginning of Paul's ministry we find his name listed behind Barnabas' yet later on, we find their names reversed showing us the spiritual growth and increase in responsibilities in Paul's life.

Full of the Holy Ghost and Wisdom:

> **And Ananias went his way, and entered into the house; and putting his hands on him said, Brother Saul, the Lord, even Jesus, that appeared unto thee in the way as thou earnest, hath sent me, that thou mightest received thy sight, and be filled with the Holy Ghost. And immediately there fell from his**

eyes as it had been scales: and he received sight forthwith, and arose, and was baptized.

Acts 9:17, 18

We saw earlier in Acts 1:4 Jesus commanding believers to wait for the baptism of the Holy Spirit. Paul was instructed by Ananias that the order to be filled with the Holy Ghost came from Jesus. As soon as Ananias prayed for Paul, he received the baptism of the Holy Spirit.

But we preach Christ crucified, unto the Jews a stumblingblock, and unto the Greeks foolishness; But unto them which are called, both Jews and Greeks, Christ the power of God, and the wisdom of God.

1 Corinthians 1:23, 24

Paul preached Christ in the power and wisdom of God. He had the ability to teach believers how to apply the Word of God to their lives.

Interview:

And when Saul was come to Jerusalem, he assayed to join himself to the disciples: but they were all afraid of him, and believed not that he was a disciple. But Barnabas took him, and brought him to the apostles, and declared unto them how he had seen the Lord in the way.

Acts 9:26, 27

Barnabas brought Paul before the apostles and testified of his honest report. Paul was having problems with his past report of persecuting the Jews. Barnabas' report to the apostles convinced them to accept Paul's ministry offices. Paul worked hard at studying and showing himself to be approved as a workman unto God.

Prayer:

> **Now there were in the church that was at Antioch certain prophets and teachers; as Barnabas, and Simeon that was called Niger, and Lucius of Cyrene, and Manaen, which had been brought up with Herod the tetrach, and Saul. As they ministered to the Lord, and fasted, the Holy Ghost said, separate me Barnabas and Saul for the work whereunto I have called them, and when they had fasted and prayed, and laid their hands on them, they sent them away.**
>
> **Acts 13:1-3**

Barnabas and Saul were called prophets and teachers. Their ministry offices are confirmed in the church as it says in verse 1. Verse 2 tells us they were fasting, praying, and ministering to the Lord when the Holy Spirit started to speak. "Ministered" used here, in the Greek, means to worship, receive, and obey. Prayer was the communication between believers and the Father God in which they received instructions regarding Barnabas and Paul's ministry. The Holy Ghost said, "Separate me Barnabas and Saul for the work whereunto I have called them." First, they worshipped God, then they received His instruction regarding Barnabas' and Paul's ministry offices. They obeyed by the laying on of hands and they were then immediately sent off to complete their assignment.

Laying on of Hands:

The laying on of hands as seen in Acts 13:3 was an acknowledgement of Barnabas' and Paul's qualifications for a particular work, setting them apart and giving evidence of those abilities.

TIMOTHY:

Paul, on his first missionary journey, travelled through Lystra where Timothy had received salvation. Timothy's mother was a Jewess receiving her salvation by the time of Paul's second missionary journey through Lystra. Paul did not use Timothy until his second missionary journey when he became Paul's travelling companion, possibly substituting for John Mark. John Mark left Paul and Barnabas on their first missionary journey to return to Jerusalem. John Mark was an attendant (server) for Paul and Barnabas (Acts 13:5).

Honest Report:

> **Then came he to Derbe and Lystra: and, behold, a certain disciple was there, named Timotheus, the son of a certain woman, which was a Jewess, and believed; but his father was a Greek: Which was well reported of by the brethren that were at Lystra and Inconium.**
>
> **Acts 16:1,2**

Paul chose Timothy after hearing of his good report among the brethren.

Full of the Holy Ghost and Wisdom:

**That good thing which was committed unto thee
keep by the Holy Ghost which dwelleth in us.**

2 Timothy 1:14

This is Paul's statement to Timothy confirming that he was baptized in the Holy Spirit.

Interview:

**Neglect not the gift that is in thee, which was given
thee by prophecy, with the laying on of the hands of
the presbyters.**

1 Timothy 4:14

"Presbyters" in the Greek refers to spiritual leaders of the church. Paul reminded Timothy not to disregard the gift that was activated by prayer, prophesy, and the laying on of hands.

Prayer:

Prayer and the laying on of hands are closely tied together in the appointment of ministry gifts (offices) in the church. Acts 6:6 and Acts 13:3 show that prayer was followed by the laying on of hands. Therefore, we can conclude that prayer preceded the laying on of hands (1 Timothy 4:14) in the appointment of Timothy to his ministry office. We can also see in 1 Timothy 1:18 and 1 Timothy 4:14 that Timothy had received numerous prophecies which assuredly followed prayer.

Laying on of Hands:

> **Wherefore I put thee in remembrance that thou stir
> up the gift of God, which is in thee by the putting
> on of my hands.**
>
> **2 Timothy 1 :6**

Timothy had received a special endowment for his mission, communicated and confirmed by the elders of the church. The gift mentioned by Paul is Timothy's ministry office (ministry of helps). We know this scripture refers to the confirmation of Timothy's ministry because Acts 6:6 states that laying on of hands follows confirmation and appointment of ministry offices in the church. We saw another example of this in Acts 13:2, 3 when Barnabas and Paul were set apart for a special work in the ministry. Timothy's gift of grace of serving motivated him toward his ministry office of helps (1 Corinthians 12:28) confirmed in the church by the laying on of hands.

15

THE FRUIT OF LOVE

The Holy Spirit comes to live inside a believer at the time of his salvation and sheds the love of God abroad in his heart (Romans 5:5). Salvation opens the way for the fruit of the Spirit (Galatians 5:22). Every Christian can and should display love, joy, peace, longsuffering, gentleness, goodness, faith, meekness, and temperance in his life.

The fruit of the Holy Spirit is the basis for the operation of God's gifts in a believer. First John 4:8 tells us God is love and he that does not love knoweth not God. Jesus Christ is God manifested in the flesh; therefore, as representatives of Jesus Christ, we should do everything in LOVE. Love is the key that produces fruit in the believer's life when he operates in God's gifts.

> **Now there are diversities of gifts, but the same spirit.**
>
> **1 Corinthians 12:14**

The Holy Spirit is in charge of the operation of the gifts (manifestations of the Holy Spirit) in the church.

And there are differences of administrations, but the same Lord.

1 Corinthians 12:5

The Lord Jesus Christ is in charge of the ministry of gifts (offices) in the church.

And there are diversities of operation, but it is the same God which worketh all in all.

1 Corinthian 12:6

The Father God works all the manifestations of the Holy Spirit through all the offices of Jesus Christ in the church. Therefore, the gifts (manifestations of the Holy Spirit) you operate in are determined by your ministry offices.

But covet earnestly the best gifts: and yet I show you a more excellent way.

1 Corinthians 12:31

Paul says believers should covet earnestly the gifts (manifestations of the Holy Spirit) that would enhance their ministry office(s). The best gifts are those that would benefit the most people. As we have discussed throughout this book, the ministry gifts are given to profit the body of Christ by bringing multitudes into the Kingdom of God. The ministry gifts (offices) are an expression of the personality of Jesus Christ. Believers are vessels that God uses to operate through. It is imperative that the body of Christ covet gifts (manifestations of the Holy Spirit) that would strengthen their ministries.

The more excellent way is to lay a foundation of love before you start seeking the gifts. First Corinthians 13 depicts the operation of love in a believer's life. "Way" in the Greek means road, indicating that believers are required to walk the love road benefiting others.

> **But the fruit of the Spirit is love, joy, peace, long-suffering, gentleness, goodness, faith, meekness, temperance: against such there is no law.**
>
> **Galatians 5:22, 23**

The fruit of the Spirit is AGAPE LOVE, and that love operates through eight manifestations.

1. JOY

2. PEACE

3. LONGSUFFERING

4. GENTLENESS

5. GOODNESS

6. FAITH

7. MEEKNESS

8. TEMPERANCE

When a believer walks in love, these manifestations will be displayed through his life.

> **Abide in me, and I in you. As the branch cannot bear fruit of itself, except it abide in the vine; no more can ye, except ye abide in me.**
>
> **John 15:4**

Jesus Christ is the vine and Christians are the branches. The branch draws life from the vine and bears fruit. Christians who are not in fellowship with the Lord Jesus Christ do not have the potential to produce fruit.

> **Blessed is the man that walketh not in the counsel of the ungodly, nor standeth in the way of sinners, nor sitteth in the seat of the scornful. But his delight in is in the law of the Lord; and in his law doth he meditate day and night. And he shall be like a tree planted by the rivers of water, that bringeth forth his fruit in his season; his leaf also shall not wither; and whatsoever he doeth shall prosper (bear fruit).**
>
> **Psalms 1:1-3**

The tree brings forth his own fruit in His season. The Holy Spirit is the water that permeates through the roots, vine, and branches enabling the tree to bear fruit at the proper time. There is a correct time for a tree to bear fruit. For example, trees are at rest in the winter and do not produce fruit. In the spring, trees bud with blossoms and in the summer, fruit is born. Likewise, the Christian will produce fruit in his season. Young Christians are not able to produce fruit because of their spiritual immaturity. Young trees need to be fed, watered, and nurtured. This is also true with young Christians. They need to be fed the Word of God and given time to grow spiritually in wisdom.

> **Come unto me, all ye that labour and are heavy laden, and I will give you rest. Take my yoke upon**

you, and learn of me; for I am meek and lowly in heart: and ye shall find rest unto your souls.

Matthew 11 :28, 29

Jesus said He would give rest to those who are laboring in their own fleshly efforts. The first question you need to ask yourself is, are you born again? If the answer is no, you need to receive Jesus Christ as your personal Lord and Savior by asking Him to come and live inside of you. If you are already born again but are laboring in your own fleshly efforts, then repent and let Jesus Christ build on His foundation. If you are a new Christian, spend time feeding on God's Word.

Trees produce fruit at the correct season with no prompting necessary. When the right season comes, the branches bear fruit. The fruit that is required to come forth from Christians is agape love. Through agape love, Jesus Christ can build ministries upon His foundation (salvation) in a believer's life.

For other foundation can no man lay than that is laid, which is Jesus Christ.

1 Corinthians 3:11

Upon salvation, the believer is required to plant himself in God's Word to learn of Him (Jesus Christ), resulting in a production of fruit in the correct season, thereby glorifying the Father God.

16

Activate Your Anointing

The anointing is a divine endowment given by the Holy Spirit, rendering believers holy and separated unto God for their particular work in the ministry. Further, the anointing symbolizes equipment (God-given gifts, talents, and abilities) for service. YES! Every believer has been anointed to activate his God-given gifts, talents and abilities.

> **But ye (believers) have an unction (anointing) from the Holy One (Holy Spirit) and ye know all things.**
> **1 John 2:20 (explanation mine).**

"Unction" is anointing and in the Greek is defined as the bestowal of divine favor or appointment to a special place in the purpose of God. It is noteworthy that the anointing reveals a knowledge concerning a believer's area of ministry. John states a believer's revelation (knowledge) regarding all things pertaining to the anointing comes with this gift.

But the anointing which ye (believers) have received of him abideth in you, and ye need not that any man teach you: but as the same anointing teacheth you all things, and is truth, and is no lie, and even as it hath taught you, ye shall abide in him.

1 John 2:27

Some believers have misused and taken this scripture out of context by arguing they do not need teaching because the Holy Spirit teaches them everything. That is not what John is saying in this scripture. Let's look at what John reveals about the believer's anointing. The Holy Spirit reveals God's plan for a believer's life through the gift of anointing. No one can tell someone else what his calling is in the body of Christ, but they can confirm what has already been spoken by God to the believer (Matthew 18:16). John was in no way telling believers that since they have the Holy Spirit they do not need teaching from others. If so, then the five-fold ministry gifts would have been given by God in vain since these ministries were given for the perfecting (maturing) of the saints. No! John was talking specifically about God's plan for the individual believer's life. The anointing abides within the believer, which permanently reveals God's ordained plan.

The Holy Spirit's gift of anointing is God's blueprint for believers. The anointing teaches believers their part in God's plan and empowers them to execute it. This gift causes believers to become good stewards of God's time. As believers are led by the Holy Spirit step by step, precept upon precept they become effective and efficient at carrying out God's plan. Believers cannot afford to have their anointing deactivated stopping the power of God from working through their lives. This would result in spiritual deafness rendering them unable to be led by the Holy Spirit in executing God's plan.

The anointing is activated by the infilling (baptism) of the Holy Spirit. Jesus commanded believers to wait in Jerusalem for the baptism of the Holy Spirit.

> **And, being assembled together with them, commanded them that they should not depart from Jerusalem, but wait for the promise of the Father, which saith he, ye have heard of me. For John truly baptized with water; but ye shall be baptized with the Holy Ghost not many days hence.**
>
> **Acts 1 :4, 5**

Jesus said to wait for the promise (Holy Ghost) of the Father. One reason Jesus commanded them to wait for the baptism of the Holy Spirit is found in Acts 1:8:

> **But ye shall receive POWER, after that the Holy Ghost is come upon you: and ye shall be my witnesses unto me both in Jerusalem, and in all Judaea, and in Samaria, and unto the uttermost part of the earth.**

"Power" used here, in the Greek, is *dunamis* defined as God's miracle working power. Jesus said when the Holy Spirit comes upon a believer, he will receive power to become His witness. In the Greek, anointing symbolizes equipment for service in association with the baptism of the Holy Spirit. The anointing is activated when a believer receives the baptism of the Holy Spirit. Let's look at our example, Jesus Christ:

> **And the Holy Ghost descended in a bodily shape like a dove upon him, and a voice came from heaven, which said, Thou art my beloved Son; in thee I am well pleased.**
>
> **Luke 3:22**

> **And Jesus being full of the Holy Ghost returned from Jordan, and was led by the Spirit into the wilderness.**
>
> **Luke 4: 1**

Jesus was baptized with water and the Holy Ghost in the river Jordan. The baptism of the Holy Spirit is a separate experience subsequent to salvation (Acts 19:2). Jesus' anointing was activated upon being baptized in the Holy Ghost, allowing the power of God to be demonstrated in and through His life. Immediately after the Holy Ghost came upon Jesus, He led Him into the wilderness to reveal God's plan for His life.

> **And Jesus returned in the power of the Spirit into Galilee: and there went out a fame of him through all the region round about.**
>
> **Luke 4:14**

Jesus returned in the power of the Spirit with a revelation of God's plan for His life on earth.

> **The Spirit of the Lord is upon me, because he hath anointed me to preach the Gospel to the poor; He**

**hath sent me to heal the brokenhearted, to preach
deliverance to the captives, and recovering of sight
to the blind, to set a liberty them that are bruised, to
preach the acceptable year of the Lord.**

Luke 4:18, 19

Jesus' anointing not only revealed God's plan for His life but
also empowered Him to execute it. Luke 4:14 tells us Jesus became
famous because of the power of God that was being demonstrated
through His life. He had the ability to preach the Gospel, heal the
brokenhearted, recover sight to the blind, and display other miracles.
Jesus is our example and everything He said or did was because of
His Father's will (John 5:30). When Jesus was baptized in the Holy
Spirit, His anointing became activated and God's plan for His life
became clear. Every step He took was guided by the Holy Spirit's
leading as we saw in Luke 4:1. Jesus fulfilled His calling by doing
the will of His Father who sent Him. The Father God revealed,
equipped, and empowered Him to execute His plan.

There are five aspects to the Holy Spirit's gift of anointing:

1. The anointing sanctifies and separates believers unto God
    for their particular work in the ministry. Acts 13:2

The Holy Ghost said in Acts 13:2, "Separate me Barnabas and
Saul for the work whereunto I have called them." The Holy Spirit
separates believers for their particular work in the ministry rendering
them holy and separated unto God. Every believer has a particular
area of ministry for which he is responsible.

2. The Holy Spirit gives the gift of anointing that activates believers' God-given gifts, talents, and abilities. 1 John 2:20

We saw this in 1 John 2:20 where John states that the anointing comes from the Holy One (Holy Spirit).

3. The anointing reveals and teaches every aspect of a believer's ministry office(s), God's plan and purpose for his life.

As we see in 1 John 2:27, the anointing reveals and teaches everything believers need to know regarding their area of ministry in the body of Christ.

4. The anointing equips, enables and empowers believers for their particular work in the ministry. Luke 4:14; Acts 1:8

The beginning of Jesus' ministry occurred after He was baptized in the Holy Ghost (Luke 4:14). Everyone noticed a change including the community in the region round about Galilee. Jesus knew the importance as well as the necessity of being baptized in the Holy Spirit. The anointing activated His gifts, talents, and abilities resulting in a demonstration of miraculous power through out His ministry. Knowing the significance of the baptism of the Holy Spirit in the believer's life, Jesus commanded His disciples to stay and wait for the Father's promise.

Jesus Christ is the same yesterday, today, and forever. Are you a disciple of Jesus Christ? The definition for disciple is one who follows another's teaching. If you are following Jesus Christ's teachings, you are His disciple. Therefore, you have the same order today as the disciples did at the day of Pentecost. You have the choice of receiving the Father's promise (baptism of the Holy Spirit) and fulfilling God's call on your life or you can continue in your own natural ability. The anointing is what makes the difference! The baptism of the Holy Spirit activates your anointing, allowing God to demonstrate Himself through your life with POWER.

5. The Holy Spirit sends believers out to fulfill their calling by activating their anointing which puts God's gifts, talent, and abilities to use. Acts 13:4

The Holy Spirit lays out the plan (blueprint) and reveals the necessary steps for believers to fulfill just as He did in Acts 13:4. Jesus said no man builds a house without counting the cost. The blueprint shows the builder how and what to build and the materials needed. Jesus Christ is the foundation of the believer's home (heart), whereas the Holy Spirit is the blueprint (revealer of God's gifts, talents, abilities) within the believer. A person building a custom home is required to have his plans (blueprint) approved. There are usually changes that occur before finishing the house but without starting, the changes would never occur. It is the same in the Kingdom of God since faith requires action. As you become involved in areas of church ministry, the Holy Spirit will be able to lead your next step.

HOW TO ACTIVATE YOUR ANOINTING

1. The Holy Spirit is the agent in sanctification as we can see in 2 Thessalonians 2: 13: "But we are bound to give thanks always to God for you, brethren beloved of the Lord, because God hath from the beginning chosen you to salvation through sanctification of the Spirit and belief of the truth." If you have received Jesus Christ as your personal Lord and

Savior, you have been sanctified and separated unto God by the Holy Spirit.

2.   The Holy Spirit gives the gift of anointing to each believer at the time of salvation. The activating of the anointing comes by the baptism of the Holy Spirit, an experience subsequent to salvation. Receiving the baptism of the Holy Ghost will activate your anointing.

3.   Revelation is an aspect of teaching. The Holy Spirit reveals God's plan (step upon step) and teaches the believer how to execute it. The only way a believer can hear the Holy Spirit reveal God's plan for his life is to step out and become involved in a local body (church). A believer's God-given gifts, talents, and abilities are for the body of Christ. Paul states in Acts 13:1 "Now there were in the church that was at Antioch certain prophets and teachers." The gifts operate in the church; therefore, the believer must become involved in a church in order to find his ministry gift(s) and place in the body of Christ. It is your responsibility to step out. The Holy Spirit cannot lead you unless you're moving and He is waiting on you to make the first step. "For precept must be upon precept, precept upon precept; line upon line, line upon line; here a little, and there a little" (Isaiah 28:10). Being led by the Spirit of God is a training process. Step out and train your spirit to listen to the leading of the Holy Spirit.

4. The only way a believer can find his equipment (God-given gifts, talents, and abilities) for service is by using them. Many believers are waiting until they see physical proof of their abilities before getting involved in the church. The equipment for service received from the Father God is activated by use. These gifts, talents, and abilities are supernatural and cannot be seen with your natural eye. When you use them they become tangible. For example, if a person called as a teacher is never involved in a church, then he would never know God's ability to transmit knowledge residing in him. When you commit to a body of believers and become involved in church, the God-given gifts, talents, and abilities are tangible. Not only can you see your gifts, talents, and abilities but so can the rest of the body of Christ.

5. The crucial key to operating in your gifts, talents, and abilities is being involved in a local church. It actually goes beyond being in a church; the question you need to ask yourself is: Am I on a winning team? There are at least five ingredients to a winning church (team):

    a. Are there souls being saved?

    b. Are there needs being met?

    c. Are there lives being changed?

    d. Is there a pastor's anointing?

    e. Are you allowed to grow and express yourself as God has created you?

Find a church that is involved in outreach and allows everyone an equal opportunity to become active in service. You are an extended outreach of your church.

Every believer has an anointing that abides within him permanently. The anointing you have received from the Holy Spirit is a divine calling. God has separated you unto Himself for a particular work here on earth. Persons and things in the Old Testament were anointed to signify holiness or separation unto God. This was a temporary anointing for a particular use and purpose of God. Today God has put the anointing within the believer, sanctifying and separating him as holy for a purpose. That purpose is to serve God with his spirit, soul, and body.

Stepping out without your anointing is like going out to play football without your equipment. Your flesh will soon realize it can't handle the punishment. The anointing is God's protection plan for believers enabling them to fulfill their calling. The gifts and callings of God cannot be taken away from the believer but it is still up to the individual to activate his anointing and use his equipment (gifts, talents, and abilities).

ABOUT THE AUTHOR AND ROGERS MINISTRIES

Susan and her husband teach the word in demonstration of the spirit and power. The heart and passion of this ministry is to win the lost, heal the sick and have believer's trained and launched into their God given destinies. Having helped equip believers in bible schools, churches, and conferences around the world, our heart is to see you, your family, and local body fulfill the call of God.

Thornwell and Susan Rogers are ordained spirit-filled ministers having pastored two churches and travel extensively domestically and internationally. Susan has been in ministry since 1980 when she became a branch of Word Ministries out of Atlanta, Georgia, founder Germaine Copeland.

Susan Rogers has an anointed teaching ministry that enables her to convey the uncompromised word of God with every day practical application and strongly confirmed with the gifts of the Spirit, especially the revelation gifts (word of wisdom, word of knowledge, discerning of spirits). Susan has written various books including "Gifts", "Selah", "Born to Laugh" and "Worth of a Woman through God's Eyes" presently being revised. Susan and her husband, Thornwell, reside in Tulsa, Oklahoma. They have a son, daughter, and three grandchildren.

Contact Susan Rogers at www.rogersministries.com. or at:

Rogers Ministries

9524 East 81st Street, Suite B 1726

Tulsa, Ok 74133

1-877-770-4469

PRAYER OF SALVATION

God loves you—no matter who you are, no matter what your past. God loves you so much that He gave His one and only begotten Son for you. The Bible tells us that "...whoever believes in Him shall not perish but have eternal life" (John 3:16 NIV). Jesus laid down His life and rose again so that we could spend eternity with Him in heaven and experience His absolute best on earth. If you would like to receive Jesus into your life, say the following prayer out loud and mean it from your heart.

Heavenly Father, I come to You admitting that I am a sinner. Right now, I choose to turn away from sin, and I ask You to cleanse me of all unrighteousness. I believe that Your Son, Jesus, died on the cross to take away my sins. I also believe that He rose again from the dead so that I might be forgiven of my sins and made righteous through faith in Him. I call upon the name of Jesus Christ to be the Savior and Lord of my life. Jesus, I choose to follow You and ask that You fill me with the power of the Holy Spirit. I declare that right now I am a child of God. I am free from sin and full of the righteousness of God. I am saved in Jesus' name. Amen.

If you prayed this prayer to receive Jesus Christ as your Savior for the first time, please contact us on the Web at **www.harrisonhouse.com** to receive a free book.

Or you may write to us at
Harrison House • P.O. Box 35035 • Tulsa, Oklahoma 74153

The Harrison House Vision

Proclaiming the truth and the power

Of the Gospel of Jesus Christ

With excellence;

Challenging Christians to

Live victoriously,

Grow spiritually,

Know God intimately.